Gardening...Naturally

Gardening... Naturally

D. X. Fenten

LINE DRAWINGS BY HOWARD BERELSON

FRANKLIN WATTS, INC., NEW YORK, 1973

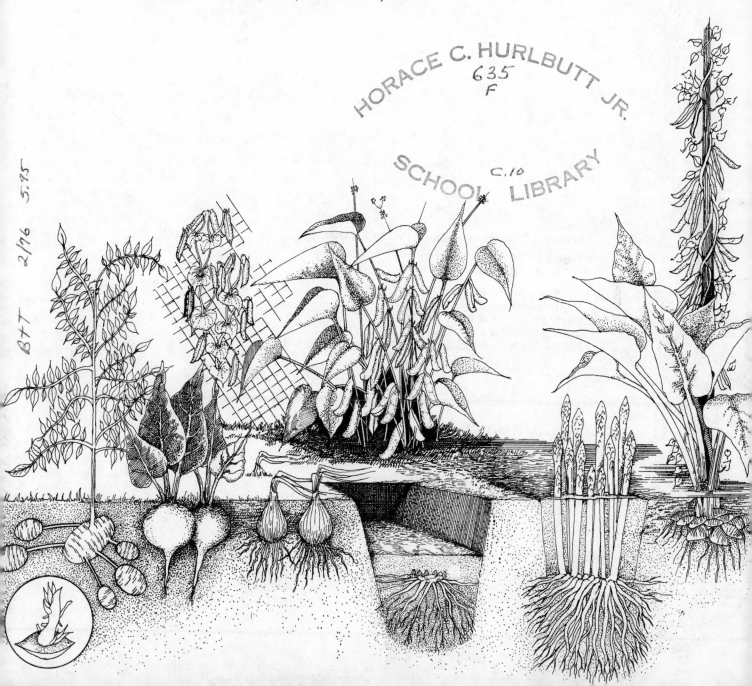

Library of Congress Cataloging in Publication Data

Fenten, D   X
     Gardening . . . naturally.

     Bibliography: p.
     1. Organic gardening. I. Title.
SB453.5.F45   635'.04'8   72-13790
ISBN 0-531-02625-6
ISBN 0-531-02338-9 (pbk)

Preface

There's something exciting about organic gardening. It's not new. It's not mysterious. It's not difficult. But there's something about it that keeps tugging at you, calling to you until you finally are compelled to try it. That's it. You've *got* to try it. Organic gardening is a way to do something "like they did it in the old days," only much better.

Maybe it's because of all you've heard from organic gardeners about their crops—the biggest vegetables, the juiciest fruits, the most colorful flowers, the healthiest trees. That's part of the call but there's more. Gardeners keep saying it's natural. It's the way nature intended. You don't have to kill something to grow something else. Everything seems to balance—take something out, put something back. There is no danger to people, pets, birds, and other living things resulting from poisonous sprays.

You are working with nature. It's up to you to find the right balance for your garden, here and now. You are doing something to make things better. You can share and balance, working with nature. Now you clearly hear the call of gardening the natural way. It finally gets to you—and you've got to try it.

Every author wants his book to have an effect. I, too, hope this book will have an effect. Hopefully, by reading it, you will be prompted to try organic gardening. With all honesty, I can say that since I have been gardening organically, I have never had such fun, such abundance, or such remarkable produce. Try it—I think you'll like it too.

Few books are one-man jobs. This book is a real "home team" effort. The "regulars" did the kind of job that only they can do. The kind of job that made this and all my other books possible. To my parents, my wife, and my children for their interest, their encouragement, their patience, their love, and their very real help in editing, typing, and proofreading, once again, thanks.

D.X. Fenten

Greenlawn, N.Y.

Contents

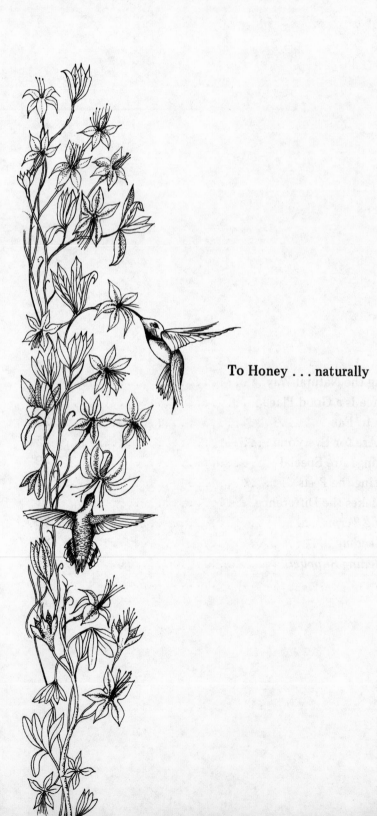

To Honey . . . naturally

CHAPTER 1

Gardening the Natural Way

Everyone can enjoy organic gardening. It's fun, it's easy, and it makes sense.

What do we mean when we speak about organic gardening or gardening naturally? Ask twelve people and you will get twelve different answers. To some, it is a very serious, very strict set of rules. To some, it is a belief, something like a religion. To some, it is a fad that is fine when it's here, but even better when it's gone.

Organic gardening is a better way to grow things. It is a way that is fair and honest—take something out of the earth, put something back into the earth. It is a way in which everything is real; nothing is fake, phony, or man-made. It is a way that uses no insecticides, miticides, fungicides, herbicides, or any other "cides" to kill insects, mites, fungi, or plants and weeds. It is a way that uses no chemicals, preservatives, or colorings. It is a way that avoids killing and, instead, encourages living. In short, organic gardening is the natural way of doing things, the way that nature would do things (and has done, that's how we learned about them) if we didn't interfere.

Let's take a look at this world of organic gardening. It includes birth and death, growth and decay, work and play. All are important to complete the circle that nature herself has set up. It is important to realize, right at the beginning, that though organic gardening is as close to nature's way as possible, even it is not perfect. Suggestions that will work in one place will not work in another. Use the suggestions and information that follow whenever and wherever you can. Mix well with common sense and a lot of care. Remember, a little is a lot better than nothing. Eighty percent is better than 50 percent, but 100 percent is the best of all and is certainly the surest road to success in organic gardening.

Gardening is easy when you know what you are doing, but even then, it requires lots of time, lots of effort, and lots and lots of patience. Almost nothing happens overnight. It takes time for seeds to sprout and then to grow and then to flower and then to bear. So, if you're going to do some gardening, be prepared to do it slowly, be prepared to do it sensibly, and be prepared to do it correctly. Because gardening is really worth doing, it is really worth doing right. Shortcuts can be good, but more often than not they lead to disappointments. Nature takes her time and everything happens as it should, so take time with your gardening.

Only a few things are "musts" for gardening. Though there are exceptions, which we'll see later, there are only a few things you really need in gardening. You must have sun. You must have water. You must have soil. And, of course, you must have seeds or bulbs to plant.

Soil, good soil, is probably the most important ingredient to successful organic gardening. If it is not the most important ingredient, it quickly becomes the most important, because it is the one ingredient over which you have the most control. There's not too much you can do about the sun—except to see that your plants get as much of it as possible. And, there's not too much you can do about water—except, again, to see that your plants get as much as they need. But, there's a lot you can do to and about your soil. You can turn very poor soil into rich soil. You can change soil that is as hard as concrete into soil that is soft and "just-right" crumbly. You can change soil that will grow almost nothing into soil that will grow just about anything.

We keep calling it soil, not dirt. What's the difference? Dirt is the stuff you get on your hands, face, and clothes. Soil, the topmost layer of the earth, is used to grow plants and is a lot more useful. Made of water, air, minerals, and organic matter, soil is so important to most plants that it can make the difference between a skinny, sickly plant and one that is big, beautiful, and healthy.

Where can you get good soil to use in your garden? In your garden, of course. Take whatever is there—good, bad, hard, soft, sand, or clay—and start adding organic matter and minerals. Sounds pretty easy when you read about it, but it must be difficult to do? You wonder where to start, what do you really add, where do you get the right stuff to add.

The best place to start getting the soil ready for planting is wherever the soil happens to be. For some this means the backyard, for others it will mean the nearest flowerpot or window box, and for still others it will mean a trip to a hardware store, nursery, or garden supply shop. Wherever you go for your soil, before you buy, test it. Pick up a handful and let it run through your fingers. The ease and speed with which the soil runs or doesn't run through your fingers will give you an idea of the soil's structure. Once you find this out, you'll know exactly what your soil needs and what it doesn't need. Then you'll be able to figure out what to add and what not to add.

The structure of the soil is very important because it determines the amount of water and food that is passed along to a plant's roots. The soil's structure also decides how difficult it is for newly germinating seedlings to push to the surface and get at the light. To make matters a bit easier for the gardener, the different kinds of soil are divided into four distinct groups—loamy soil, sandy soil, clay soil, and adobe soil.

Loamy soil is made up of sandy soil and clay soil mixed with lots and lots of humus (organic matter). It is just about perfect for planting and growing everything—flowers, vegetables, trees, shrubs. When you take a handful of loamy soil, it crumbles into different sized pieces and moves evenly through your fingers. You'll be able to tell by the feel that this kind

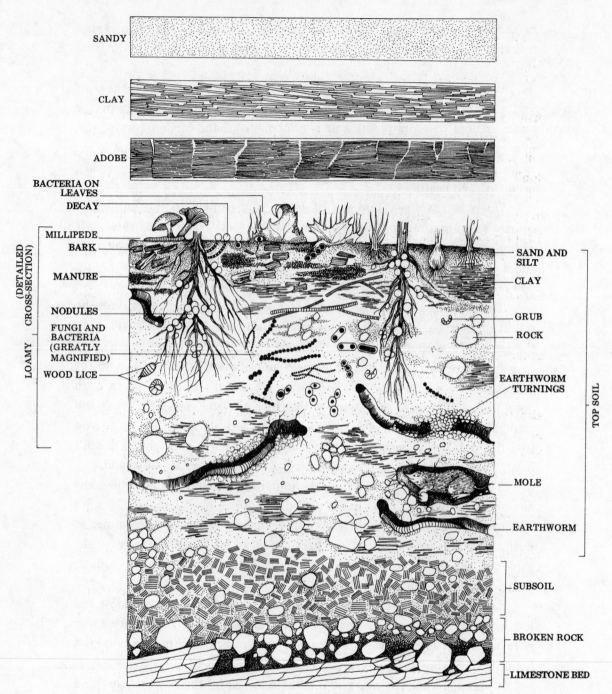

SANDY

CLAY

ADOBE

BACTERIA ON
LEAVES

DECAY

MILLIPEDE

BARK

MANURE

NODULES

FUNGI AND
BACTERIA
(GREATLY
MAGNIFIED)

WOOD LICE

(DETAILED
CROSS-SECTION)

LOAMY

SAND AND
SILT

CLAY

GRUB

ROCK

EARTHWORM
TURNINGS

MOLE

EARTHWORM

TOP SOIL

SUBSOIL

BROKEN ROCK

LIMESTONE BED

Structure of the four different types of soils.

of soil will hold the right amount of water and plant food and pass them along to your plants. If you've got loamy soil, you're all ready for the next step. If your soil is not loamy, you will have to make it so.

Sandy soil is very light, doesn't hold together, and allows water and plant food to drain right through. Run it through your fingers and, like beach sand, it runs through very quickly. Many plants can be grown in sandy soil, but to keep them growing well you must feed them very often. If you don't, the plants will suffer, for the plant food washes right through sandy soil and only feeds the roots as it passes by. To make sandy soil into loamy soil you must add all sorts of organic matter, such as peat moss, humus, and manure—more about that later.

Clay soil can be a problem both in the spring when you're ready to plant as well as later on in the year after the seeds have been planted. Because it is very heavy and sticks together, like clay, this kind of soil holds lots of water in the spring, making it almost impossible to break up so you can sow your seed. When it finally does dry out, a crust forms and water cannot get through to the plant's roots. The cure for this kind of soil is plenty of organic matter and some sand, all mixed thoroughly and deeply.

Adobe soil is not only the most difficult kind of soil to work with but also the most difficult kind of soil to remedy. Adobe soil is clay soil, only more so. Found in our country's hottest, driest areas, adobe soil is very heavy clay soil that cannot take in any of the rain that falls, not even the very small amount that usually falls in these desert-like areas. The soil gets hard, almost like concrete, and then it cracks. The only way to improve this soil enough so that more than just the few kinds of plants that like this soil can grow is to add some sand and loads and loads of organic matter. Then add some more organic matter and then, when you think you're all finished, add some more.

The organic matter is vital to good gardening. It is the most important part of your bargain with nature—take something out of the soil, put something back into the soil. There are so many different kinds of organic matter that the best way to identify them is as any part of anything that once lived. This includes animals and vegetables. It includes any wastes or by-products (leftovers) from animals and vegetables. Many of the things you throw away as garbage can and should be put back into the soil to feed it and keep it in good shape for growing plants.

For plants to grow and be healthy, for flowers to bloom and have beautiful blossoms, for trees to bear large, delicious fruit, and for vegetables to be worth eating, they need oxygen and carbon, which they get from the air, and hydrogen, which, along with more oxygen, they get from water. They also need nitrogen (N), phosphorous (P), potassium (K), and thirteen other plant foods, all of which must come from the soil. The easiest but not the best way to put these nutrients, or plant foods or fertilizers, into the soil is to pour it out of a box or bag. There are at least one hundred and fifty different kinds of chemical, man-made fertilizers that you can buy and use on your soil. They will do the job, but you can never be sure what else they will do. Nature never intended man to pour all sorts of chemicals into her soil.

Nature's way is to replace what is taken from the soil with something that is pretty much the same. Flowers, fruits, vegetables, and plants are organic so it makes sense that a similar type of organic matter must go back into the soil. Leaves, weeds, grass clippings, and other once green things make fine additions to the soil. They are easy for most gardeners to get and best of all they are usually free and yours for the taking.

If you live near a farm or any other place that has animals (even the biggest cities have riding academies or stables), you'll be able to get a very good fertilizer and soil improver—manure. Just ask the owner's permission and usually you'll be able to get as much of this excellent organic material as you can cart away.

People who live near certain kinds of factories can get other excellent organic materials free for the asking. Factories that turn cottonseed, soybean seed, and other seeds into oil are often pleased to let you take away the "leftovers." After the oil is pressed from the seeds the waste must be carted away—you'll do both yourself and the factory a favor by doing the carting. But, of course, always ask first—there is always the chance they may be organic gardeners too.

Sewage sludge is a problem for some towns and a money-maker for others. Some towns sell it and some towns give it away. Find out where you can get some for your garden (of course, free is by far the best) and use it liberally.

If "free" organic matter is not available, you must pay the price at local garden supply stores. There you'll be able to buy bags of soil feeders and improvers, including cottonseed meal, animal manures (sheep, cow, horse, and chicken in a variety of forms), fish and blood meal and fish emulsions. All are wonderful for the garden.

Most of the organic matter listed is rich in nitrogen. To add phosphorous to your soil, ask your local garden supply man for some bone meal or very finely ground phosphate rock. To add potassium, get some of the other rock dusts and powders, including that made from granite and potash. If you have a wood-burning fireplace or know someone who does, take the ashes (hardwood is best) just as they come from the fireplace, spread them over the soil, and then spade them into the soil to add natural potassium.

Not a word has been said thus far about the organic gardener's best friend—compost. Since it's the best, it has been saved for last. Whenever there's talk of organic gardening there's also talk of compost. This decayed organic matter is the special favorite of organic gardeners for a great many reasons—it is natural (made from once living things), it is easily available (you make it or, really, it makes itself), it's part of nature's circle (it returns to nature what you take from nature), and it's free.

Everyone should have a compost heap. Those gardening in window boxes, pots, or other containers can build very small heaps; those with outdoor gardens, especially vegetable gardens, should prepare a large compost heap adequate for their needs. Not only does the compost heap give you beautiful, rich, dark, crumbly humus that feeds and improves your soil, it also helps to solve part of the garbage problem.

The instructions that follow are for those people with large gardens who can use lots of compost. If you have a smaller garden scale the heap down until it fits your needs. Start out by collecting all the organic matter you can find. Grass clippings, leaves, kitchen "throwaways," such as coffee grounds, eggshells, vegetable skins and so forth, weeds and other organic matter are fine for making compost. Even though bones, wood, meat scraps, fat, cloth, and similar items are organic, they should not be included in the

7

compost pile; they take too long to decompose and are often more trouble than they are worth.

Spread your collection of organic matter into a 6-inch-deep layer on bare ground that measures about 4 feet by 4 feet. If you run out of these organic materials and need more, remember that your local lumber yard (sawdust), supermarket (vegetable wastes), and processing factory (shells) and hulls from seeds and nuts, spent hops, grapes, and others) will probably be delighted to have you help yourself to their "garbage." As you add materials to the compost heap, be certain everything is in small pieces, no larger than a quarter (25-cent piece) for the quickest, finest compost.

Push several poles into the ground through this first layer of compost-to-be and smack the poles a few times with a hammer until they are standing firmly. Make a fence of wire for a neat compost pile, but it's not really necessary unless animals begin to rummage through the compost. Toss a 3- or 4-inch layer of animal manure (if no farms are nearby, back to the garden supply store) around the poles, then add a 3- or 4-inch layer of good soil to the pile. Add some wood ashes, ground limestone and other rock powders—whichever are available. Water the entire pile thoroughly but don't drown it. All of this makes one complete layer, so now you are ready to start all over again. Second layer, assorted "garbages," manure, good soil, ashes, rock powders, water. Repeat again and again until your compost heap is about 4 feet tall; now pull out the poles (you've been piling stuff around them all this time); the holes will allow air to circulate in the pile.

After allowing the heap to "do its own thing" for about a month, turn as much of it as you can with a spade or a pitchfork, water it, and once again, leave it alone. After another month, turn and water it again. Wait another month (that's three) and you'll have fantastic, beautiful humus.

So far you haven't done much gardening. Here's your chance to start. If you are gardening in containers, begin mixing your soil. Take several hand-fuls of humus (compost) and mix thoroughly (using your hands) with the soil in the pot. Continue to add compost until you have soil that feels just right for planting—not too heavy, not too light, but just right—rich and crumbly.

Making a compost pile.

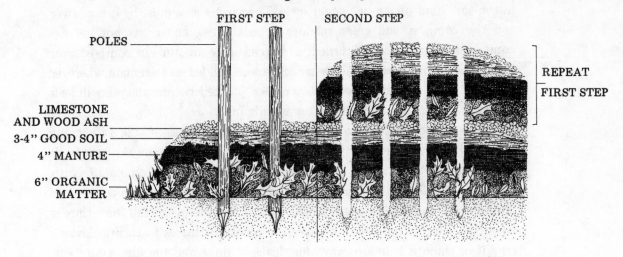

FIRST STEP SECOND STEP

POLES

REPEAT
FIRST STEP

LIMESTONE
AND WOOD ASH
3-4" GOOD SOIL
4" MANURE
6" ORGANIC
MATTER

Completed compost pile, fenced in with wire.

Those of you who are gardening "out back" can also do some "playing in the soil," but on a much larger scale. The garden area must be turned over and the compost and green manure (weeds, grass, and other not yet decomposed organic matter) turned in. Spread large amounts of compost over the area for your garden. Allow weeds, grass, and leaves to remain wherever they are. If your garden area has ever been planted before, the job will be a lot easier. If not, roll up your sleeves and dig in.

Use a spade or fork to dig out about 6 to 8 inches of soil. Lift it out (one clod), turn it over so top is bottom and bottom is top and throw it back down. Be sure to include a good portion of compost and green manure with each spadeful. Turn the garden over and the compost in, one clod at a time until the whole area has been turned. If this is done in the fall (best time is when the weather is cool and there are plenty of leaves to turn in), don't rake it or smooth it in any way. Just leave it alone and the sun, wind, rain, and snow will work on it all winter while you're cozy and warm in the house. Then, when spring comes your garden will be ready for planting. The compost will feed the soil and improve its structure and the green manure will decompose and do the same thing. All you do in the spring is rake and you'll be all set to plant the seeds that will produce the most beautiful flowers and the most delicious vegetables you've ever dreamed about.

CHAPTER 2

Every Place Is a Good Place

The question "Where should I do my gardening?" comes up almost as often as "What should I plant?" Unfortunately, there is no simple answer to either question and only you can do the planning and make the decisions. Please note that the planning comes first. It might seem hard to wait when you are excited and want to get started with the real thing—digging and planting—but, here, as with other things, patience and the results make the waiting worthwhile.

Before doing anything else, consider the many possibilities open to you. If you live in the country and have a large piece of property, selecting a spot for your garden should be fairly simple. If you live in the suburbs and have more limited space, the choice begins to get more difficult. If you live in the city, of course, you are limited to window boxes, pots, and assorted containers. Wherever your planting is going to be done, give yourself the best chance for success—do it out in the open, on level land that's in sunlight for most of the day.

Start small in both planning and practice. Gardening is another of the situations in which it is much better to do a little bit perfectly than to do a "so-so" job on a lot. Everything in the catalogs and at the garden stores looks so beautiful and so delicious, you'd like to try them all. But remember that everything requires attention—lots of work and lots of care. Also, if you start small the first year you only make a few small mistakes and can learn from them for the following year. By starting small, you can learn and let your garden grow along with your experience year after year.

If you are doing your planting in containers, be sure to select those that are large enough to allow the plants to grow. To make large containers portable, put them on dollies (small four-wheeled carts) and push them wherever you want them to go. There is almost no limit to the kinds of things that you can use for containers—small poly coffee cups, plastic drinking cups, waxed milk containers (from ½ pint to gallon size), plastic bleach bottles, tin cans, and many, many more, including ordinary clay pots your local florist may be throwing away. Look around your neighborhood and in your local stores. Watch for something that is inexpensive or free, will hold soil, will not rust or fall apart, and can have a drain hole poked into its bottom. Many food stores will be glad to give you large plastic, metal, and treated-paper containers that once held bulk food products. All you have to do is ask for them. Poke a hole or two in the bottom of the container, add a layer of gravel, coarse sand, or small pebbles before putting in the soil, and you're ready to begin.

A few other quick suggestions for successful container gardening. Always water thoroughly, but don't drown the plants. When the soil looks and feels dry, water; otherwise leave the plants alone. When you water, wash the leaves and pour on plenty of water. Let it soak through for a few minutes and then pour off any extra water. Feed the plants with an organic fertilizer (fish emulsion is fine for this) about once a month in summer, about once every other month in the winter. Don't overfeed. Read the directions on the fertilizer package carefully and follow them exactly. Select plants for growing in containers that do not grow too large and do not have to be repotted too often. Careful plant selection can mean the difference between plants that become a chore and plants that are a delight.

Container gardeners, town and city people and others without land on which to have a garden, should look around their area for other gardening possibilities. Vacant lots, gardenless soil around public buildings, such as churches, synagogues, schools, courts, police and fire stations, offer excellent opportunities to the gardener. Do a little asking around your neighborhood and you might discover some land on which to garden. Offer to give the owners or people in charge some pretty flowers, vegetables, or even fruit from the garden (as a way of saying thank you) and you'll probably have a deal. They supply the land, you supply the labor, and you both have a good deal. Remember also that a few containers of beautiful, colorful flowers placed in special spots for special people can go a long way toward getting you what you want. Go ahead, try it. You might find everybody likes it.

Whether your garden spot is on your property or on someone else's, try to find a spot that is as close as possible to your house and a supply of water. Dragging tools, hoses, and assorted other equipment long distances can quickly become a bother. Look for a spot that gets plenty of sunlight. At least eight hours a day of sunlight is a must, and the more sunlight the better. Avoid areas that are shaded by buildings or trees if you can. Sunlight is a key ingredient. Find an area that is level. Be certain the ground you pick is not too close to hedges, shrubs, or large trees. Their roots will compete with the roots of your plants for food and water and, of course, the larger roots of the trees and hedges will win.

That brings us to the second question "What to plant?" which has several answers. First of all, plant only what you really want to plant. Plant only what you will enjoy caring for, working with, and, in the case of fruits and vegetables, those that you and your family really like to eat. Sounds like common sense but you'd be surprised how many people don't do it. Your next consideration is the amount of space you have. And, finally, you must consider whether your plants will do well where you are planting them.

For window boxes and containers select dwarf flowers and vegetables. For small plots choose plants that are upright and compact, but not neces-

What to plant? Flowers and fruit for the windowsill garden, vegetables for out-of-doors, are good choices.

CORN

POLE BEANS

PEAS

PUMPKIN

MELON

CABBAGE

CAULIFLOWER

DWARF FRENCH MARIGOLD

GERANIUM

DWARF ORANGE

IMPATIENS

MINIATURE ROSE

sarily dwarfs. For large garden areas, you're the boss and what you choose to plant will be governed only by the amount of time and energy you want to spend. To give you an idea, melons, pumpkins, cucumbers, and other running crops take up lots and lots of space, but they don't require too much attention. Corn, because you need at least five rows to get good pollination, also takes up quite a large amount of space but requires a bit more attention. Peppers are pretty compact, as are the members of the cabbage family, peas, beans, and others. The same situation is true with flowers. Roses need a good sized space and lots of care. Marigolds need less space and less care. Impatiens need very little space and almost no care.

Check the catalogs for "mature height" and "growing characteristics" before you buy plants or seed. Careful reading will give you a very good idea of what your plants will look like, how wide and how tall they will grow, and sometimes, even how much care they will need. It is much better to find out as much as you can about the plants you are going to grow before you plant them, rather than the hard way, once they are growing.

When your list of "things to grow" is complete, start thinking about whether you want to plant seeds or seedlings. Most nurseries have a wide selection of young plants, called seedlings. Many people prefer seedlings, while others prefer starting their own seedlings from seed indoors and then transplanting them outdoors into their own gardens or containers. Since many more varieties of seeds are available than seedlings, you have a much wider selection from which to choose if you start your own seedlings. Also, it is wonderful fun to watch and care for the seeds as they sprout and then begin to take on a form you can recognize. Another attraction of starting your own seedlings is that your gardening fun begins during the winter, while the snow is still on the ground, in the warm comfort of your home.

Here's how to get the best, strongest seedlings to transplant into your garden.

1 Buy fresh, name brand seed. Don't ever look for bargains when it comes to buying seed. Seed is very inexpensive, so if you hope to end up with the best, you've got to start with the best. You can start many flowers from seed indoors and then transplant the seedlings into the garden. You can

do the same with vegetables except for peas, beans, corn, and carrots. Planting directions on the package will tell you if the seed can be transplanted or if it is best started from seed sown directly into the garden.

2   Do your selecting early. Many other people are doing the same thing you are. If you hope to get exactly what you want, do your shopping early whether from a mail order catalog or at a local store. In January or February many stores charge a lower price for seeds.

3   Buy only natural seeds. That is, seed that is exactly the same as it was when it came from the plant. Many seedsmen treat their seeds with a variety of chemicals to protect them and the seedlings that will come from them. Start off right, organically, without any chemicals or treatment.

4   Get everything ready long before you are going to do any sowing. Start sowing seed indoors about eight weeks before you want to transplant the seedlings outdoors. To determine the date for outdoor planting, find out the last day frost may be expected in your area, add about one more week for safety's sake, and then count backward eight weeks and you'll know exactly when to start the seed indoors.

5   Prepare a mixture of equal amounts of sphagnum peat moss, coarse sand, and potting soil. If you don't want to mix it yourself you can buy "seed starting soil" ready to use at garden stores and nurseries. Decide what kind of containers (usually called "seed flats") and how many you will need to use to start your seedlings. A low sided plastic tray or wood box is a good choice, or you can use little individual pots. If you don't have enough or can't get them from friends or neighbors, these too can be bought in all sizes and shapes at the same stores. Ask for seed flats, fibre board flats, plastic trays and pots, or peat pots. Fill each container about halfway with the soil mixture.

6   Pour water into the half-filled containers until the soil mix is thoroughly wet. If there is any extra water, pour it off (but only after you are positive the soil mix is soaked through and through).

7   To make a furrow or other indentation in the soil mix to hold the seeds, use a pencil, a dowel, or a small stick. If there is room in the container, place the stick flat on top of the soil mix. Press it gently into the soil

and then lift it off. A shallow furrow will remain in the soil ready to receive the seed.

8   Place the seeds carefully into the furrow. Space them exactly as directed on the seed package. Don't throw in a few extra seeds for good measure. Spacing is important if you are to have strong, healthy, sturdy seedlings.

9   Spread additional soil mix over the newly sown seeds. Use only a very thin layer, not more than about 1/4 inch thick. Sprinkle on some water but do it very carefully. Splashing or pouring the water will knock your carefully planted seeds all over the container.

10   Next, prepare an individual greenhouse for each container. This "greenhouse," a plastic bag, keeps moisture in and softens light rays to provide more even and more complete germination. For the good of the ecology, you will want to reuse a plastic bag, if you have one, that covered your newly dry-cleaned clothes. Knot one end, carefully slip in the container, and then knot the other end. If bags from the dry cleaner are not available, use food storage bags or even those for roasting meat or poultry.

11   Put your new little greenhouse in a nice warm spot and leave it there until the seeds have sprouted. Do not put the greenhouse in a sunny window or anyplace else where there is very strong direct sunlight. You may have quick seed germination but you may also have some beautifully cooked seedlings. Keep the greenhouse in a warm (but not hot), sunny (but not too sunny) spot for no more than about six hours each day.

12   This step is the most difficult of all—watching and waiting. That's it—you do nothing but watch and wait. When most of the seeds have sprouted, you can get back into action. When the sprouts are about one inch tall turn the pots completely around each day so that the young seedlings do not start to lean too much toward the sun. Keep the container inside the plastic bag until the seedlings are about 1 1/2 inches to 2 inches tall, then remove the bag.

13   Watch for the seedlings to get their first set of true leaves. You can identify these leaves, even though they are small, because they are the first ones to look like the full-sized leaves on a grown-up plant. Tomato

plants start to look like tomato plants, marigolds start to look like marigolds, and so on. When the first leaves appear, it is time to transplant the seedlings into individual pots, either peat pots, growing cubes, plant flats, or other containers. The little seedlings need to be separated now so that they can grow without crowding.

Transplanting is simple if you are careful, take your time, and treat your seedlings as if they were as delicate as a spider's web, because they are. If you are the least little bit sloppy or careless now, all your earlier work can be ruined, leaving you with nothing but some soggy soil and a few seedlings.

Gather all the things you will need to do the job in one spot: larger pots or containers, soil mixture, water, a pointed stick (called a dibble) or pencil—and a very steady hand.

Fill the pots halfway with the soil mix, wet it, and make a hole with the dibble. Then, still using the dibble, push it into the soil of the seedling container. Push the point into the soil mix about one inch from the seedling and aim it down and toward the base of the roots. The angle of the dibble should be about 45 degrees. Gently hold the seedling with one hand and press down on the dibble with the other to pop out the seedling.

Carefully put the seedling into the hole you made for it in the new pot's soil mix. Allow the seedling to go down into the hole only as far as the first leaves, don't cover either set of leaves. Gently pack the soil around the seedling and put the pot in a bright window. Water every other day and turn the plants one quarter turn each day.

After several weeks your seedlings will be ready for transplanting outdoors in the garden (we'll see how that's done shortly), or for transplanting into any number of containers for growing indoors and outdoors. If, for example, you are planning to fill a window box, all you have to do is select those plants you think will look and do best in your window box, prepare the box, and put in the plants. In the case of a window box, it is important that you choose dwarf varieties or compact growers that are neither too tall nor too wide when fully grown. Since very little space is available in most window boxes or planters, plants that grow tall or wide make the whole thing look messy.

BOSTON FERN

SPIDER PLANT

CALADIUM

STRAWBERRY BEGONIA

IVY GERANIUM

LANTANA

FUCHSIA

Hanging baskets can be one of the handsomest ways of growing plants, indoors and out.

Be certain your window box is sturdy and has drainage holes about the size of a dime in the bottom. Lay a piece of wire screen over the holes and then cover the screen and the bottom of the box with about an inch of small pebbles. Fill the box to about one inch from the top with rich, dark, compost-loaded garden soil. The same steps are taken for window boxes, planters, and even for hanging baskets.

And, they are really something to try—hanging baskets. If you want live plants but have limited indoor and outdoor space, hanging baskets may just do the trick. They are easily made, inexpensive, and beautiful. Use any attractive pots you happen to have or buy some at variety, hardware, or garden stores. Attach a strong wire or chain to holes you have made in the pot's rim at three points, each point the same distance away from the next. Draw the wire together evenly above the pot and knot the three strands together. Hang the unit from a cup hook you have screwed into a solid piece of wood in the ceiling, window frame, or other place. Make sure the hanging basket won't drip on your furniture, rugs, or floor. Hang a clay saucer (sold with pots in garden and variety stores) under your pot if you think it will drip. Or take the hanging basket down and water it in the kitchen sink, letting it drain thoroughly before rehanging it.

Plan ahead again when selecting plants to go into your hanging basket, planter, or window box. Do you want flowers, greenery, or both? If your choice is greenery for your window box, put the tallest plants in the back and the shortest in front. A planter or hanging basket usually can be seen from all sides, so put the tallest plants in the middle and the shortest all around the outside. Use the same scheme if you prefer flowers—with still one more suggestion. Although colorful flowers are lovely to look at, too many colors and too many flowers are unattractive, confusing, and not at all pleasing to the eye. Limit yourself to one or two kinds of flowers and colors in a single container. If you decide to use more than one kind of flower and more than one color be sure they go well together.

If you decide to use greenery and flowers in the same container, put the green plants at the rear of window boxes to serve as background and in the center in hanging baskets and planters. Just about all the plants you choose for planters and window boxes should be upright growers; plant vines or other plants that grow down only at the front edges of the boxes. For hanging baskets, you can choose from among the many pretty vines and cascading kinds of flowers.

Everywhere you plant, indoors and out, you'll get pleasure from seeing what you can do with your own time, effort, and imagination, without the help of any man-made chemicals. There is a special delight when you've raised your plants from seed to full, adult beauty, naturally. And, there is an almost unbelievable delight that comes from eating something right out of the garden that started from a tiny seed. It's a treat that must not be missed.

CHAPTER 3

Delicious to Eat

Vegetables. Big, beautiful, juicy vegetables. They go with the word and thought "organic." Though you can and should grow everything organically, most people think only of things to eat when they think of organic gardening. For those people, we'll first look at the world of unbeatable eating; a little bit later, we'll look at the colorful, beautiful, and aromatic world of flowers.

It is possible that some people will disagree, but growing vegetables is one of the most exciting adventures anyone can have. If there is anything more exciting than growing vegetables it has to be harvesting and eating them. Think about it. The whole of nature's life cycle in a very short time: seed to plant to fruit to seed, right before your eyes.

Let's take the healthy seedlings of the last chapter and do what has to be done to get them growing and producing in the garden. About a week before you are going to put the seedlings into the garden give them a small step to help them on their way. The difference between living in your warm, windless, protected window and living in the cold, windy, open outdoors takes quite a bit of getting used to for the young seedlings. Prepare them for the rugged life of early spring by doing some "hardening off." That is, slowly but surely, prepare the plants for the tough outside world by making them tougher. Stop all watering and place the seedlings outdoors in a protected spot or into a cold frame (a large box that has been sunk into the ground, which is open on the bottom and covered with a top of plastic or glass). If you keep your seedlings indoors, all snug and warm until the minute you put them into the garden, they will probably not be strong enough to make it through all the temperature changes, wind shifts, and other changeable outdoor weather.

Once the seedlings are hardened off (one week to ten days is fine, two weeks are better) you're ready for the final transplanting. This is the big one—the one that really counts. Goof here and all the work, the watching, the waiting, and the care go down the drain. Do a good job here and you are on your way to the best tasting vegetables you've ever had.

Check your seedlings as you take them from the cold frame or other hardening-off spot. Only the healthiest, sturdiest seedlings should be transplanted for they are the ones with the best chance of surviving the shock of transplanting.

Single seedlings growing in individual pots are ready to go into the ground just as they are. If they are growing in peat pots or growing cubes, simply wet the plant, the soil, and the organic pot thoroughly and plant.

Seedlings growing in plant flats, usually six, nine, or twelve to a flat (most nurseries do it this way), must be "blocked" before you plant them. A few days before you plan to put your seedlings into the garden, cut the soil in the flat into cubes. Use a sharp knife and make your cuts just the way you would cut through a flat cake or pan of brownies. Make careful cuts, first in one direction and then in the other, through the soil and the roots. Each cube should have one seedling, roots, and soil. Try to make each cut so the seedling will have as much soil and as many roots as possible.

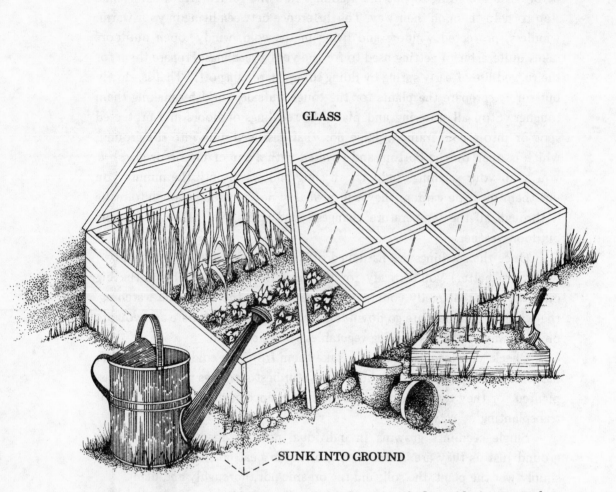

GLASS

SUNK INTO GROUND

Seedlings growing in a cold frame, sunk in the ground. One side is propped open to let the seedlings harden off.

To give your seedlings every chance to make it past the first few days, do all your transplanting on cloudy days or late in the day after the sun has gone down. A very hot sun beating down on seedlings just after they have been transplanted may dry them out and kill them.

This is where your advance planning pays off. Since you have already figured out where each seedling should go, depending on the full-grown size of the plant, you are now ready to plant. You have also weeded and freshly spaded up your garden plot. Now, get a piece of string to use as a guide in making straight rows. Pull the string taut and make your planting holes all along the string. Be certain the plants are set far enough away from each other. Seedlings look very small when you plant them, but they grow quickly—give them plenty of room. Measure your shoe and use it as a guide—that way you always have an accurate measure with you. Dig the holes wide enough and deep enough to hold the seedling, soil cube, and roots. Use a trowel or, if you have one, a bulb planter to make the holes. Make sure the hole is deep enough to hold the seedling's root ball, deep enough so that the top of the root ball is just slightly below the surface of the soil in the garden.

To protect your seedlings as long as possible, first dig all the holes and then put a handful of humus (compost) or dehydrated cow manure into each hole. The manure is supposed to be odorless, but from our experience—if the wind is blowing your way—wow! Place a single seedling into each hole and water. Use enough water to wet down the seedling and the sides of the hole, but not enough to make the hole into a tiny swimming pool. Replace the soil that you dug out of the hole. Do not pack down the soil, but press it gently with your fingers, so that no air pockets are left beneath the surface (air pockets would dry out the roots). Water again, and go on to the next seedling.

After you have planted all the seedlings, think about the temperature predicted for that night. If radio, television, or newspaper weather reports predict falling temperatures, protect your newly planted seedlings with hot caps (which you can buy), fruit baskets (from local markets), tin cans (you know where to get those), or pointed hats made out of newspapers (that you can make yourself). These should be placed over the young seedlings every night that you think it might be cold. When the temperature rises permanently, stop using the caps. Now your seedlings are finally on their own.

The following special suggestions should make your chances for success with certain vegetables even better. To keep it simple, vegetables are grouped according to the way they are planted:

1 From seedlings started indoors—cabbage family, eggplant, lettuce, pepper, and tomato.

2 Seedlings started indoors or hills outdoors—cucumber, melon, pumpkin, and squash.

3 From seeds sown directly in the ground—beans, beets, carrots, corn, peas, radishes, spinach, onion sets, and potato eyes.

4 From crowns or roots—asparagus and rhubarb.

Grow the members of the cabbage family that you like, depending upon whether or not they like your local climate. Cabbage does well in all but the hottest areas, while broccoli likes it a bit cooler, and Brussels sprouts even a bit cooler than that. Plant the seedlings a little deeper than you do other plants to give added support to the large heavy heads. All cabbage family members are spaced 18 inches apart in rows 30 inches apart. Watch your watering of this group and keep it steady. If you let the soil become dry and then start to water again, the heads will probably split wide open.

Another vegetable that likes steady water is the black beauty, eggplant. Plant seedlings about 30 inches apart each way, water well, and watch the large, firm fruits grow. These plants do especially well in areas where the weather is very warm.

Lettuce, on the other hand, bolts (goes to seed and becomes very bitter) as soon as the weather turns hot and dry. Plant it in the garden very early in the spring, just as soon as the soil has dried a bit and you can dig a seedling hole. See that the heads are spaced 18 inches apart in rows 24 inches apart. Water often and very well.

Peppers are a lot like tomatoes but take up a lot less room. Plant peppers about 18 inches apart in rows 24 inches apart after you are certain there is no danger of frost. Water well, but not so much that the plants are left standing in water.

Plant tomatoes at least 3 feet apart each way in late spring or early summer. Water well, but don't let tomato plants stand in water either. It's a good idea to stake your tomatoes. Use either single poles or "A" shaped frames and attach the plant with cloth or plastic covered ties that will not cut the branches. When you stake you may get fewer tomatoes, but the ones you get will be clean, beautiful, and stand a much better chance of not attracting bugs or diseases.

Cucumbers, pumpkins, squash, and melons are wonderful plants to grow, but if left to roam they will take up lots and lots of space. For the very small garden they are often, unfortunately, out of the question. Medium to large size gardens can handle them, but even there, they should be trained to go where you want them to go. Train them up a turkey wire fence, wooden trellis, or strong string line and you'll have wonderful fruits and vegetables—and space for other plants.

All of the Group 2 vegetables (page 26) can be grown from seed sown directly in the ground or from seedlings started indoors and then transplanted out into the garden. When all danger of frost is gone, sow four or five seeds in a single hole called a hill. Space the hills about 6 feet apart. When the seeds have sprouted, thin out, or pull up and throw away, all but two or three of the strongest looking seedlings. Water heavily all during the growing season. If the seedlings are started indoors in organic peat pots, you'll give yourself a fine head start toward earlier harvesting.

A lot of favorite vegetables are on the list of seeds to be sown directly in the garden. With the exception of corn, peas, and beans, each of the following will give you a single vegetable from a single seed and each takes up very little space. Try some of each, or at least those that you really like, and plant enough to allow you to reap a worthwhile harvest.

The bean family offers you a choice between snap or green beans, pole beans, and lima beans, and all grow pretty much the same. Soak the seed in water overnight and plant in late spring in soil that does not become hard and crusty. Space the seeds 3 inches apart in rows 3 feet apart. Make your holes about one inch deep, drop one seed in each hole, cover with good soil or compost, and water thoroughly. If you have planted a variety that needs support (such as pole beans), provide wire or mesh netting for them to climb or individual poles to which you can tie the plant.

Cross-section of a healthy vegetable garden.

A – TOMATO
B – CABBAGE
C – BROCCOLI
D – LETTUCE
E – PEPPER
F – CUCUMBERS ON TRELLIS
G – STAKED GREEN PEAS
H – CARROTS
I – POTATO

J – POTATO EYE, READY TO PLANT
K – PEAS ON WIRE FENCE
L – BUSH LIMA BEANS
M – STAKED POLE BEANS
N – BEETS
O – ONIONS, TOPS BENT
P – TRENCHED ASPARAGUS CROWNS
Q – ASPARAGUS READY TO CUT
R – RHUBARB

If you really like beans and want plenty of them all through the summer, plant a row or two every other week, at least through to the end of August. Harvesting will be staggered and you'll be loaded with the best beans ever.

Beets are a little bit more fussy than other vegetables, so if you want good results, give them what they like. For example, as a root crop, beets like soil that is loose so the roots can grow. Hard soil will keep the roots from spreading out, and all you'll get will be skinny, little beets. While you're loosening up the soil with extra compost add some extra ground natural limestone. It helps make the soil less acidy and that's what beets like.

Plant beets early in the season. They grow much better when the weather is still cool. Plant beet seeds no more than one inch deep and about 1½ inches apart in rows 18 inches apart. When the seedlings are about 6 inches tall, thin them out so that the beets are at least 3 inches apart. Don't throw away the thinned out seedlings. Try them in a salad—they're delicious.

Carrots too need loose, compost-rich soil. If your soil is lumpy and full of rocks, the carrot roots (the part you eat) will be lumpy too. Plant carrot seeds in early spring in rows about 18 inches apart and no more than half an inch deep. Space the seeds about 1½ inches apart when planting, then thin to about 3 inches apart when the seedlings are 6 inches tall. Mark carrot rows carefully because the seed takes a long time to sprout and you might pull them out thinking they are weeds. A good idea is to drop a few radish seeds, which germinate quickly, into the row to act as markers.

If you have the space to plant corn, do it. There is nothing in the world that tastes as good as corn fresh from the stalk, cooked and eaten immediately. Because corn is wind pollinated, not insect pollinated, it is very important that you plant it in several short rows standing side by side instead of in one or two long, straight rows.

Plant the seed early in the spring just as soon as all danger of frost is gone. You can sow the seed in either of two ways—rows or hills. If you like rows (called drills for corn), put one corn seed in each 1-inch-deep hole. Space these holes 6 inches apart in rows 3 feet apart. Thin to about 1 foot apart after seed has sprouted.

To plant in hills, drop five or six seeds into a single hole spaced about 3 feet away from the next hill. Thin to three or four plants in each hill after the seed has sprouted. Keep the plants well watered as you wait for your first ear of corn. By sowing seed every few weeks for the first month or so, you will give yourself fresh corn, ripe and ready for picking, over a longer period of time.

Peas are another treat that is hard to beat when eaten freshly picked from your own garden. Use the same suggestions as those given for beans and all will be well. Don't forget to give them something to climb on—that's when they do their best.

Radishes make every gardener look as if he had not only a green thumb but nine other green fingers as well. Radishes are easy to grow and grow very quickly, so give them a try. Plant them very early in the spring and every week for the next several weeks. Plant the seed about half an inch deep, one inch apart in rows one foot apart. Pick the radishes just as soon as they are mature (about three weeks after planting) or they get very bitter and woody.

Start spinach as early in the spring as the soil can be worked. Sow spinach seeds about 1 inch apart and thin to about 3 inches apart. Use the thinned seedlings in salads for a wonderful green treat. Water well all through the growing season and harvest the plants while they are young and tender.

If you want to put some bite in your life, try onions. Though they can be grown from seed and seedlings, your best bet is to use sets (small dry onions grown a year earlier and available in garden stores and some hardware stores). Plant the sets about 1½ to 2 inches deep, 3 inches apart, pointed part up, in rows about 18 inches apart. Do your planting very early in the spring just as soon as you are certain the soil will be very loose and crumbly. Water thoroughly as they grow. When the tops get very tall, start to show seed on top, or get yellowish, bend them to the ground, but don't tear them off. This allows the plant's bulb (the onion part) to grow larger since the plant no longer needs to support the tops with food.

Another slightly different but very interesting vegetable to grow is the potato. Not too many people grow them in home gardens, but those who do are delighted. Plant in late spring in soil that is extra rich in compost and manure. If you can, prepare the soil and dig in the compost and manure the previous fall.

Potatoes are grown from pieces of special potatoes called seed potatoes. They are different from eating potatoes and are the only ones you should use. Cut each seed potato into cube-shaped pieces so that each cube has at least one eye or, if possible, two eyes (the little nubs on the potato). Dig a trench that's about 6 inches deep and a couple of inches wide and space the potato pieces in it about 18 inches apart with the eyes up. Cover with rich soil, but not all the way to the top of the trench. Leave about a 2-inch ridge in the trench. When the potatoes sprout and are about a foot tall, add the rest of the compost until the trench becomes level with the garden soil. Water thoroughly but not too much. After the leaves have wilted, the potatoes can be dug up. You must dig very carefully so as not to cut into any of the delicious tubers (potatoes). Cook any number of different ways and you'll rave about home-grown potatoes.

Last, but far from least, are two vegetables grown from crowns, or roots—asparagus and rhubarb. Both are planted just once and grow fantastic stalks year after year after year. With a little care, the original crowns can give you tender stalks for as many as fifty years.

Though asparagus can be grown from seed, it's a much better idea to use one-year-old crowns with at least a 12-inch-long root spread. And, like potatoes, prepare the soil with lots and lots of compost and manure the previous fall.

Dig a trench about 18 inches wide and 18 inches deep. Fill the trench with about 12 inches of compost and place the crowns, with their roots spread out, about 18 inches apart, on the compost. Cover with about 2 inches of compost and water well. Add more compost throughout the growing season until the trench and soil are level. No matter how tempted you may be, do not cut stalks the first year. Cut them the second year and every year after that.

Rhubarb too likes lots of compost and manure, but, unlike asparagus, it can be planted anytime from mid-fall to early spring. Just set the crowns about 4 feet apart, cover with more compost, and water well. Don't do any picking the first year, but enjoy harvesting the second year. *Never* use any part of the leaves of the rhubarb plant. They contain *poison*. Cut and use only the stalks and enjoy tender, juicy rhubarb.

If you have any space left in the garden after you have planted all these vegetables, try some herbs. Select the ones your mom likes to use in cooking and then choose a few more to try. Follow the directions on the seed packet.

Herbs are an organic pest repellent, too, when planted with vegetables; see page 63.

There are, of course, other vegetables than those listed here, but these are most people's favorites. Some special varieties of these vegetables will give you a starting point, but after the first year, don't limit yourself to these—always keep trying new kinds, new varieties, new vegetables, new herbs to help you find your favorites and to enjoy the excitement and fun of gardening.

Special Vegetable Varieties to Try

Broccoli —	Cleopatra, Calabrese, Italian Green Sprouting
Brussels Sprouts —	Long Island Improved, Jade Cross
Cabbage —	Copenhagen Market, Danish Ballhead, Red Acre (red)
Cauliflower —	Snowball, Perfection
Eggplant —	Black Beauty, Early Beauty Hybrid
Lettuce —	Salad Bowl, Slobolt (leaf); Great Lakes, Big Boston (head)
Pepper —	California Wonder, Ruby King (sweet); Long Red Cayenne (hot)
Tomato —	Supersonic, Better Boy; Golden Jubilee (yellow) Pixie and Patio (container); Red Cherry and Tiny Tim (cherry)
Cucumber —	Smoothie, Burpee Hybrid, Burpless Hybrid
Melon —	Muskmelon, Early Honey Dew, Crenshaw
Pumpkin —	Big Max, Sugar, Jack O'Lantern
Squash —	Acorn, Banana, Hubbard, Butternut, Turban (winter); Patty Pan, Crookneck, Cocozelle, Zucchini (summer)
Beans —	Tender Pod, Topcrop (bush); Pencil Pod (wax) Kentucky Wonder, Tendercrop (snap); Fordhook (lima); King of the Garden (pole lima)

Beets —	Detroit Dark Red, Early Wonder, Ruby Queen
Carrots —	Tendersweet, Nantes Half Long, Imperator
Corn —	Golden Cross Bantam, Surecross, Honeycross, Country Gentlemen, Silver Queen
Onion —	Bermuda, Sweet Spanish, Yellow Globe
Peas —	Lincoln, Little Marvel, World's Record
Potato —	Irish Cobbler, Early Gem, Sebago, Kennebec
Radishes —	Cherry Belle, French Breakfast, Icicle (white)
Spinach —	America, Virginia Savoy, Bloomsdale Long Standing
Asparagus —	Mary, Martha, and Waltham Washington
Rhubarb —	Valentine, Cherry, Victoria

Midget Varieties for Indoors and Outdoors

Cabbage —	Little Leaguer
Carrots —	Tiny Sweet, Sucram, Short 'N Sweet
Corn —	Golden Midget, White Midget
Lettuce —	Tom Thumb, Bibb
Pea —	Mighty Midget, Dwarf Gray Sugar
Squash —	Gold Nugget
Tomato —	Tiny Tim
Watermelon —	New Hampshire Midget

CHAPTER 4

Flowers Are for Everyone

Flowers are truly beautiful and are loved and appreciated by all kinds of people. Flowers are for everyone, everyplace, everytime. No matter what the occasion—happy, sad, usual, unusual, sports, or party—flowers are always appropriate. They are easy to grow, fun to grow, and well worth the time and effort needed to bring them to their point of beauty.

Easy, yes. But still, you must know what you are doing.

For example, you must know if the flowers you want to plant are annuals, biennials, perennials, or something else. You must know how long they bloom, when they bloom, and the color of the blooms. And, there's lots more to know.

Just about all flowers fit into one of the three groups just mentioned—annuals, biennials, perennials; those that don't are grown from such interesting things as bulbs, tubers, corms, and rhizomes. Those in the first three groups are there because of the way they grow. Those in the last group are there because they grow from something special. There are, of course, exceptions to these groupings caused by certain climates and conditions, but there are enough "regular" varieties to think about without worrying about the "exceptions."

Annuals are perhaps the easiest to understand and the simplest to grow. They take only one year to go through a complete life cycle—planted in spring, they bloom in summer and die in fall. This means that an annual must be planted each and every year if you want that particular flower each and every year. A few annuals will reseed themselves and grow again the next year without any help from you, but most annuals need your help (to reseed) if they are to grow again the following year.

Biennials take a bit longer to bloom than annuals. Planted in the summer, they are alive but dormant through the fall and winter and start to grow again in the spring. They bloom during the second summer and set seed and die in the fall. So, though they do not really need two years to bloom, they do need two summers.

Perennials usually live long lives. Planted in the spring, they grow and bloom in the summer and then wither in the fall. The next spring they grow again and then bloom and wither again. If you plant perennials you can be sure of at least two years' worth of flowers and usually many more.

All the flowers grown from bulbs, tubers, corms, and rhizomes are really perennials (they come back year after year after year) but are discussed separately from the other perennials for a special reason. Unlike other seeds, which get their food from the soil, bulbs take their food along with them when they are planted. Another important point to remember is that bulbs and corms are planted with the flat side down and the pointy side up. Tubers (you remember, potatoes) are planted with the eyes up as are rhizomes. If you should plant these "seeds" with their growing points upside-down, you'll have a hard time getting buds, if any at all.

In planning your flower garden follow the same suggestions given for vegetables and add a few more. Here too, make sure you will have enough room for the adult plants. If they are going to be a permanent part of the grounds and not cut (for flower arrangements in the house), plant them so they will grow in a pleasing arrangement. Flowers for cutting should be planted away from the house because after the stems have been cut and the flowers removed, what is left certainly doesn't look very attractive. Plant fewer flowers, fewer varieties, and fewer colors for more enjoyment. Remember to check the size, color, and growing habits of all the flowers you plan to grow. Care at this point will assure you of a beautiful flower garden instead of what could become a very colorful mess.

Because annuals are by far the easiest flowers to grow, many people "plant 'em and forget 'em." Like anything else worth growing, however, they're worth growing properly. Plant them in soil that has been prepared with lots and lots of organic matter. Feed your soil with well rotted animal manure. Water thoroughly while the plants are growing and pull the weeds as soon as they sprout. Mulching (more about this important part of organic gardening on page 50) will cut down on the amount of weeds and weeding, will keep the soil at an even temperature for the best growth, and will keep moisture in the soil.

Since most annuals are grown from seed, they can be planted either directly in the garden or indoors in a container and transplanted later outdoors. Either way the directions are the same as those given for vegetables. As mentioned earlier, some annuals go against the rules and do their own reseeding each year. With these plants all you have to do is give them a good home and let them do their own thing. They will set and sow seed each year and grow in the same area year after year. Included in the group of reappearing annuals are:

Ageratum*	Dianthus (Chinese Pink)	Pansy
Baby's Breath (Gypsophila)	Four O'Clock	Petunia*
	Gaillardia*	Poppy
Bachelor's Button	Larkspur*	Portulaca
Calendula (Pot-Marigold)	Love-Lies-Bleeding (Amaranthus)	Snapdragon
Clarkia		Strawflower
Cockscomb (Celosia)	Lupine	Sweet Alyssum
Cosmos*	Marigold*	Zinnia*

will bloom following spring-summer

37

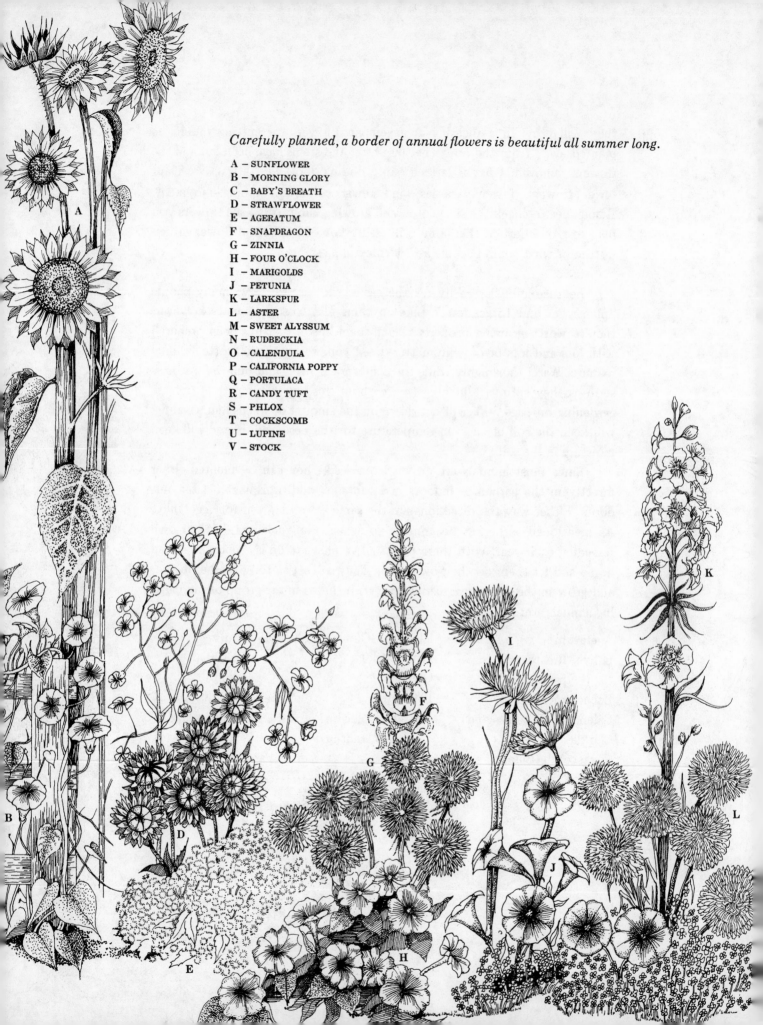

Carefully planned, a border of annual flowers is beautiful all summer long.

A – SUNFLOWER
B – MORNING GLORY
C – BABY'S BREATH
D – STRAWFLOWER
E – AGERATUM
F – SNAPDRAGON
G – ZINNIA
H – FOUR O'CLOCK
I – MARIGOLDS
J – PETUNIA
K – LARKSPUR
L – ASTER
M – SWEET ALYSSUM
N – RUDBECKIA
O – CALENDULA
P – CALIFORNIA POPPY
Q – PORTULACA
R – CANDY TUFT
S – PHLOX
T – COCKSCOMB
U – LUPINE
V – STOCK

With careful planning, your planting of annuals can give you many months of beautiful flowers. Choose from the list that follows according to the month the annual will bloom. If you choose carefully, you can have a different flower, and a different color, in bloom every month.

Selected Annuals According to Month of Bloom

May	Candytuft —	white, lilac
	Pansy —	yellow, purple
June	Baby's Breath —	pink, white
	Dianthus —	many colors
	Lupine —	blue
	Poppy —	red, pink
	Portulaca —	many colors
	Rudbeckia —	yellow
	Stock —	white, blue
	Sweet Alyssum —	white, violet
July	Ageratum —	blue
	Calendula —	gold
	Clarkia —	rose, purple
	Coreopsis —	yellow
	Four O'Clock —	pink, white
	Impatiens —	white, pink
	Larkspur —	many colors
	Marigold —	gold, red
	Morning Glory —	purple, blue
	Nasturtium —	yellow, red
	Petunia —	many colors
	Sunflower —	gold
	Zinnia —	many colors
August	Amaranthus —	red
	Aster —	many colors
	Phlox —	white, pink

	Snapdragon —	many colors
	Strawflower —	white, red
September	Bachelor's Buttons —	blue
	Cockscomb —	yellow, red
	Cosmos —	many colors

Though there are fewer biennials than annuals or perennials, the ones that do exist are too beautiful to be ignored. Try some and see if you don't agree. Because they are transplanted very easily, they can be started from seed indoors and then moved outdoors or they can be sown directly into the garden or container where they are to grow. Keep in mind that biennials prefer lots of sunlight and soil that is very rich and very full of compost. Take care in watering, for though these plants do enjoy and grow well in moist soil, they do not like being left with wet feet for too long a time. Remember that biennials need two growing seasons to flower so don't look for anything more than healthy leaves the first year.

Some Colorful, Popular Biennials

Canterbury Bell —	many colors
English Daisy —	white, pink, red
Forget-me-not —	white, pink, blue
Foxglove —	red, purple, white
Hollyhock —	many colors
Iceland Poppy —	white, red, yellow
Pansy —	many colors
Sweet William —	red, pink
Wallflower —	red, yellow

If flowers are for everyone, then perennials are certainly for everyone. There are so many different flowering perennials, not including trees, shrubs, and bushes (aha, you didn't know they were considered perennials), that it is hard to imagine not being able to find dozens that suit you and everyone else. And they come in all colors, all sizes, all shapes, and all fragrances. And if that's not enough, they are also very, very economical. One packet of seeds will give you flowers that come back year after year after year.

Because perennials do come back again and again in the same place, be sure you prepare the soil before you plant them. Dig down into the soil about 2 feet, turn it over and replace, along with plenty of composted organic matter and manure. In the following years, remember to feed your perennials to keep them healthy and blooming. The two best times to fertilize are early spring and early summer; later feeding will cause new young growth that will almost certainly be killed off by early winter weather. Carefully dig some compost and some manure into the area all around your plants. Make sure you do not go down too far with your shovel or spade, otherwise you may damage the plant's roots.

Most perennials do well in sunny areas but there are some that enjoy a shady spot. If your garden area gets less than six to eight hours of sunshine each day, try some of the following: Balloon Flower, Bleeding Heart, Candytuft, Christmas Rose, Meadowrue, Monkshood, Phlox, Plantain Lily, Primrose, Speedwell, Virginia Bluebell.

Just about all perennials thrive when they receive sufficient water. If there has been little or no rainfall in your area, you must help nature out. See that your plants get a thorough watering at least once a week and a bit more in very hot, dry weather. If you're going to do a little sprinkling, don't bother. Too little water sprinkled on the soil's surface draws the roots to the surface and seriously damages a plant. Water well or don't water at all (and don't plant either). But too much water can also be a hazard. Very few perennials like to go to sleep with wet feet. Water must get to the roots, but too much water can drown plants by crowding out the oxygen that the plants also need.

As with vegetables and annuals, perennial seeds can be sown directly in the ground or you can start them indoors and transplant seedlings into the garden. Seedlings can also be purchased at your local garden store or nursery. After your perennials have been growing for several years in the same spot they will need some extra attention. If left alone, they will become very dense, will compete for water and food, and will produce fewer and fewer blossoms. Before this happens, do some dividing and transplanting. That is, actually dig up a plant, and cut the roots into pieces, and then replant as separate flowers. For plants that bloom in the spring, divide in the fall. For plants that bloom in late summer and early fall, divide in the spring.

Do all the dividing carefully and quickly. Try not to damage any more of the roots than absolutely necessary. Use a sharp knife, make your cuts cleanly, and do not tear. As you work, cover the exposed roots with a wet towel, piece of cloth, or thoroughly soaked wad of peat moss. Plant as soon after dividing as possible and water often until the plants have taken hold.

As with the annuals, you can get month after month of beautiful, colorful blossoms from your plants if you plan and select carefully. Choose from the perennials that follow for the monthly bloom that will blend best in your garden:

Selected Perennials According to Month of Bloom

April	Alyssum —	yellow
	Candytuft —	white
	Primrose —	many colors
	Virginia Bluebells —	blue
May	Bleeding Heart —	Pink
	Columbine —	many colors
	Jupiter's beard —	white, crimson
	Meadowrue —	white, lilac
	Phlox —	white, pink
	Red-Hot Poker —	yellow, red
June	Balloon Flower —	blue, white
	Daylily —	many colors
	Everlasting —	white
	Monkshood —	blue
	Pentstemon —	red, purple
	Spurge —	yellow
	Statice —	pink, blue
	Sundrops —	yellow
	Washington Lupine —	many colors

July	Astilbe —	pink, white
	Clematis —	white, blue
	Delphinium —	many colors
	Plantain Lily —	mauve, white
	Sneezewort —	yellow
	Speedwell —	blue, white
August	Chrysanthemum —	many colors
September	Anemone —	pink, white

Anyone who has ever gardened knows the wonder of bulbs. Anyone who has never gardened but intends to should be certain to include some of the flowers from the wonderful world of bulbs in his planting. As mentioned, there are bulbs, corms, tubers, and rhizomes, and though there are differences (that you can easily see when you pick one up), all varieties are simply food storage centers for underground stems from which the next season's plants will grow. So, for our purposes, we'll call them all bulbs.

As with everything else in gardening, buy only from reputable dealers, either locally or by mail order. Don't look for bargains. Except on very rare occasions, you get what you pay for. Learn as much as you can about the bulbs before you buy them. Check on bulb size, flower size, color, planting time, blooming time, and growing habits. The more you know about your bulbs and what to expect from them, the fewer will be your disappointments.

Two things are especially important if your bulbs are to grow and bloom for many years: correct planting depth and good drainage. Bulbs that are planted too deep in the soil or too near the surface usually result in few flowers and much disappointment. Planting depth is determined by the size of the bulb—the larger the bulb, the deeper it must be planted. Each bulb variety has a different planting depth. In almost all cases the correct planting depth for a particular bulb is indicated on the bulb package. If the depth is not listed, you can figure it out: bulbs over 2 inches in diameter (across) are planted at a depth of three times the diameter (that is, if it is 3 inches across, you would plant it three times three or 9 inches deep); bulbs under 2 inches

Flowers grown from various kinds of "bulbs" come back year after year.

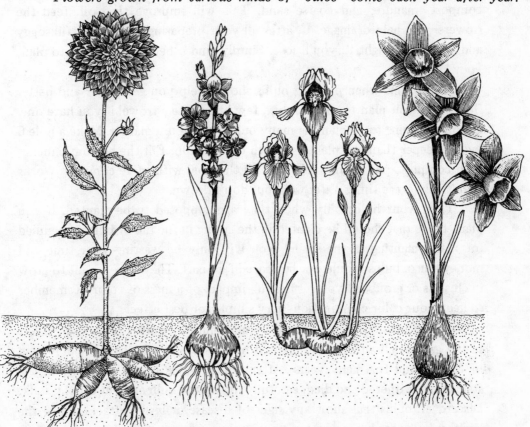

TUBER—DAHLIA   CORM—GLADIOLA RHIZOME—IRIS BULB—JONQUILL

in diameter are planted at a depth of four times their diameter. The depth of the planting hole is measured from the top, not the bottom, of the bulb to the surface of the soil.

Though they are not very fussy about the kind of soil in which they grow, bulbs are stubborn about good drainage. If the ground in which you plant your bulbs is too wet for too long, the bulbs will rot. When you prepare the soil for your bulbs (a year ahead is best) spade in plenty of compost, manure, and coarse sand. This will improve the soil, feed the flowers—and help drainage. If, after all your preparing, the soil is still soggy and wet, don't fight it, you'll lose. Simply find a better, drier spot to plant your bulbs.

A few tips when planting bulbs should help you get bigger and better flowers. If you plan to plant only a few bulbs, use a trowel if you have one. If you are going to be planting many bulbs, get a bulb planter. Make a hole 6 inches deeper than the planting depth of the bulb. Fill the bottom 6 inches with compost, put in the bulb, and fill the hole with more compost. Works beautifully every time. Water well, but don't drown.

Plant your bulbs only when they are supposed to be planted. If you plant bulbs that should be planted in the spring in the fall or bulbs scheduled for a fall planting in the spring, you will only be wasting your time and money. Also, bulbs should not be spaced far apart. They were meant to grow in clusters or groups so you get the full impact of a mass of color. Remember to keep your color combinations very simple for best effect.

Spring planted bulbs are called tender bulbs because they will die if left in the ground all winter. Fall planted bulbs are hardy bulbs and can remain in the ground for many years. After tender bulbs have flowered and the stalks have withered and died, carefully dig up the bulb and cut off the stalk. Discard all bulbs that show any signs of disease or insect attack. Allow the healthy bulbs to dry in the sun for two days. Then store them in damp peat moss until spring. Gladiolus are an exception—they do best in a mesh bag in a cool, dry spot (no peat moss or anything) until planting time in the spring.

If your hardy bulbs begin to crowd, dig them after flowering. They can be replanted right away or stored in a cool, dry place until fall.

Some bulbs can be "forced" to grow indoors, but that's for the next chapter. For now, here's a list of bulbs for outdoor growing. Each kind of bulb has different varieties, colors, and sizes within the single family. Try as many as you can and you'll complete your fun with flowers the natural way.

Selected Bulbs According to Month of Bloom and Planting Time

February	Crocus Aureus —	orange	*fall*
	Crocus Chrysanthus —	white, yellow	*fall*
	Eranthis —	yellow	*fall*
	Galanthus —	white	*fall*
March	Anemone —	many colors	*fall*
	Chionodoxa —	blue	*fall*
	Crocus Biflorus —	many colors	*fall*
	Hyacinth —	many colors	*fall*
	Leucojum —	white	*fall*
	Muscari —	blue	*fall*
	Tulip —	many colors	*fall*
April	Fritillaria —	many colors	*fall*
	Narcissus —	white, yellow	*fall*
	Daffodils —	white, yellow	*fall*
	Jonquils —	white, yellow	*fall*
	Pushkinia —	blue, white	*fall*
	Scilla —	many colors	*fall*
May	Camassia —	blue	*fall*
	Iris —	many colors	*fall*
	Lilies —	many colors	*fall*
June	Allium (Chives) —	lavender	*fall*
	Canna —	red, yellow	*spring*
	Spider Lily —	yellow	*spring*
July	Tuberous Begonia —	many colors	*spring*
	Galtonia —	white	*spring*

47

	Gladiolus —	many colors	*spring*
	Polianthes —	white	*spring*
August	Acidanthera —	white	*spring*
	Tigridia —	red, yellow	*spring*
September	Dahlia —	many colors	*spring*
	Tritonia —	red, yellow	*spring*
October	Colchicum —	purple, lilac	*fall*

CHAPTER 5

Some Things Are Special

Gardeners always have something to do. A bit of planting and transplanting, a little looking, perhaps some watching, maybe some watering, and even a little weeding. There is also careful trimming, tall staking, choosy cutting, and joyous harvesting. Every day is definitely a "doing" day for gardeners.

But, though many gardening jobs are enjoyable and fun to do, they are really "everyday" kinds of things. Things that are very important but not really very special. What about gardening's special projects and activities? There are so many of these special things you can look forward to in gardening they are almost too numerous to list and are really bound only by your own imagination and ambition.

Here are some gardening projects that are exciting and some that are plain, some that are beautiful and some that are quite ordinary, some that are colorful and some that are drab, and some for indoors and some for outdoors. Try them all and then decide whether or not these are indeed very special projects.

Several times up to now we have spoken about mulches and mulching. So now let's find out what it's all about. To put it simply, next to compost, mulch is the organic gardener's best friend. And, that's usually where you find mulch, next to compost. Mulch is a triple threat and more. It is a helper. It is a saver. It is a friend. It is a layer of easily gotten material (usually organic but sometimes not) that is put on the soil all around vegetables, trees, shrubs, and flowers. When it is put down in a thick enough layer, mulch will keep down weeds, keep moisture in the soil, keep the soil temperature even for best growth, keep vegetables off the ground and out of water puddles, and protect the plants against many kinds of weather damage. Eventually the mulch, if it is organic, will improve the soil and even feed it a bit.

Like many of the materials used in composting, mulching materials are all around us, are easy to find, and are often free. As a matter of fact, some of the best mulching materials are a nuisance to their owners and they will be delighted if you offer to cart them away. Most homeowners (who don't know the value of their "garbage") bag their leaves and grass clippings and throw them away. Offer to take this "garbage" off their hands and you'll have excellent mulch. Scout your neighborhood, see where else you can get free mulch—straw, hay, pine needles, ground corncobs, wood chips, and many, many other organic substances. If "freebies" are not available, you can buy mulching materials at your local garden shop. Some excellent mulches are peat moss, tree bark, wood nuggets, cocoa bean hulls, and various kinds of straw and hay. All of these are organic materials, all can be plowed or turned into the soil after the growing season, and all add to the soil, even while they are mulching, because they start to decompose as soon as they are put into place.

Nonorganic mulches, including sheeted black plastic, aluminum foil, fabric scraps, gravel, stones, and pebbles, can also be used, but they should not be plowed or turned into the soil because they do not decompose.

It is difficult to say which mulching job is most important, but unless you enjoy crawling around on your hands and knees, the use of mulch to eliminate weeding will probably get your vote. With any of the mulches in place, most weeds cannot get through, and you will save yourself plenty of time-consuming, backbreaking, dirty, nonproductive work.

The best time to put man-made mulches such as black plastic, aluminum foil, and newspaper layers into place is just before you put the seeds or seedlings into the well-prepared soil. Rake the soil smooth and dig two shallow trenches just slightly narrower than the width of the mulch you are using. Lay out the mulch so its sides fall into the two trenches. Hold the mulch down temporarily as you go along with heavy stones or bricks placed about 4 or 5 feet apart. After the mulch is in place, remove the stones and replace them with the soil that you dug out for the trenches. This will anchor the mulch on both sides of your planting area. Punch holes in the center of the mulch with a pointed stick (make sure the holes are spaced carefully, according to what you are going to plant) and plant your seeds in the holes. If you are planting seedlings make the hole with a tulip bulb planter and place one seedling in each hole. Refill the hole with rich soil and that's it—go on to the next.

Spreadable mulches are put into place after the seedlings have been planted. Immediately after all planting is completed, water the entire area thoroughly. Spread a thick layer of mulch all around the seedlings and water the newly mulched area. A few thoughts on the thickness of the mulch layer. Your layer of mulch should neither be too thick nor too thin. With a proper thickness, light rains and normal watering will get through to the soil. When the mulch is too thick, obviously, the water cannot get through and is wasted. Your mulch layer of grass clippings, leaves, hay, or straw should be 3 to 4 inches thick. Heavier mulches, including wood chips, tree bark, peat moss, and cocoa bean shells, do the best job when about 2 inches thick.

Mulching saves hours and hours of work—the kind of work that is no fun at all. How about using some of that "saved" time on an indoor project that's work but is also lots of fun? Build a large, specially lighted planter for home or school that will allow you to grow a wide variety of plants and flowers all year long.

Before you do any building, do plenty of thinking and planning. If you

51

A properly mulched garden is easy to take care of. In the back of the garden, a compost pile has mulch for the flowers along the fence, the rows of rhubarb, and root vegetables. Rock and gravel is used to mulch the dwarf fruit tree.

In the seed bed, black plastic sheets are used as mulch. They are spread out over the soil and weighted down. Holes are poked in the sheet for seedlings to sprout through. Plastic also keeps weeds away from the staked tomato plants.

figure carefully and correctly, the unit you build can be used as a room divider, a special plant display stand, or a very special place, tailor-made for growing and keeping plants.

Decide where you are going to put the planter and how large it is to be. You can probably build small planters yourself, but if you decide on a very large one, get some help from a parent, school custodian, or shop teacher. Do not try to do any of the electrical work without the help of an adult, preferably one who is either an electrician or one who really knows what he is doing.

If your planter is being made for use at home make sure it will fit and will not be in the way. If it will be used at school, for a hallway, classroom, or library, do not set it in a traffic aisle where students will have to go around it. Do not place the planter near heating ducts or doors that open to the outside.

Choose a spot that has enough natural light or plan to supply the necessary light with fluorescent or other lighting fixtures. Be certain also to choose a place that will not be ruined by a drop or two of spilled water.

With your helper, build your planter large enough to hold the plants you have decided to grow. Use wood or other materials that you know will last a long time. Plywood makes a solid, trouble-free planter. Put a waterproof liner—metal that has been treated so it will not rust—inside the planter. If you can't make a liner yourself, you can either have one made at a local metal shop or line the planter with heavyweight polyethylene plastic. If you are making a large planter, remember it will be very heavy when filled with soil. If it is to be moved from place to place be sure it is on wheels. Make sure the wheels will roll over both carpet and tile floors.

Because many indoor planters are kept in places where there is not enough natural light, fluorescent bulbs are needed. If your helper knows how to work with electricity, this is his part of the job. If not, be sure you use the services of a licensed electrician. Tell him what you want, and what you want it for, and he will put in the right fixture and number of special fluorescent bulbs to do the job. Also, if you have not yet decided what you are going to plant ask him how much light the equipment will provide so that you can decide which plants will grow best in your planter.

Fill the bottom of the planter with large-size gravel. Place your plants in clay pots on the gravel in an attractive scheme. Move them around, try them here, there, raise and lower them until you have the arrangement that most pleases your eye. Fill the area around the pots with sphagnum moss, marble chips, redwood or pine bark nuggets. Cover the tops of the pots with mulch and water thoroughly.

Select the plants that do best with the kind of light you have. Leafy plants need light only from the top, but flowering plants do best when they get light from the top and at least one side. Remember, too, that some plants need a lot more light than others. Some plants that are appropriate for planters and the amount of light needed by each are:

Low Light	Medium Light	High Light
Chinese Evergreen	Rex Begonia	Wax Plant
Dracena	Peperomia	Kalanchoe
Dumb Cane	Anthurium	Aloe
Philodendron	Aluminum Plant	Begonias
Snake Plant	Spider Plant	Piggyback Plant
Norfolk Island Pine	Bromeliads	Pothos
Cast Iron Plant	Cissus	Ivy
Arrowhead Plant	Syngonium	Fiddle Leaf Fig
Gold Dust Plant		

Here's another outdoor project that will give you pleasure, will help the ecological balance in your area, and might even make you the town hero. After all, who else can give the town a hundred beautiful trees at absolutely no cost?

Next fall, as you pass a particularly beautiful oak tree (or many other kinds of trees that produce large numbers of seeds), stop for a few moments and collect a small bucketful of acorns. When you get them home, count out about 200 acorns and put them aside. Find a small plot of ground to use as a nursery. It can be at your own home, a vacant lot, or, if you ask permission (you might make it a class project), on school grounds. At this stage of your own nursery project all you need is a spot about 5 feet by 5 feet.

Summer annuals grown for a school garden show.

Dig out your planting spot, turn the soil or whatever else was there under (throw out anything that's not organic), and add as much compost and manure as you can. Put some turkey wire or other wire mesh all around the nursery plot so that about one foot of the wire is in the ground and one foot is above the ground. If you do not protect your nursery in this way, you will not have a nursery for long—you will have, instead, a very nice feeder for squirrels, chipmunks, and other assorted rodents. Later, after you have planted, cover the planted area with another piece of wire mesh.

After the nursery has been prepared and protected, plant your acorns. Use a string to keep your lines straight and plant the seeds about 3 inches deep and about 4 inches apart in rows 6 inches apart. Cover with more compost, water well, and mark the area so that it will not be disturbed during the winter and also so you will be able to find it again in the spring.

Seeds, such as acorn, require a cold winter after they are planted for springtime germination. Since some seeds require more than one year to sprout, many more seeds than you want or expect must be planted. In the spring, check your nursery and see how many acorns have sprouted. Put a layer of organic mulch around each seedling, water well, and watch them grow all summer. In the fall, after the leaves have turned brown and the trees are dormant, dig each one out and transplant it into a larger area that you have prepared with liberal doses of compost and manure. They will probably have grown about 2 to 3 feet. Plant the seedlings just a bit deeper in the ground than they had been growing. Each seedling should be about 1 foot away from the next one in rows 3 feet apart. A few more than one hundred seedlings could be planted in an area about 18 feet by 18 feet. Put some stakes in the ground near the larger young trees and tie the trees to the stakes with cloth, thin plastic-covered wire, or anything else that will not damage the tree's tender bark. The stakes will support the young trees during the strong winds of winter. Water your transplants well, mulch, and, again, let the young trees rest for another winter.

Allow the seedlings to grow all the next spring and summer and get ready to transplant them once again in the fall. This time though, the transplanting will be final. Offer the trees to your town parks, churches, synagogues, or schools. Tell them the trees are free and that you and your friends will plant them as a gift. It will help to make your town a better, more attractive, cleaner, healthier place to live. If your experiment is a success, the people who received your gifts might ask for more. Put a little variety into your next tree nursery. Plant some horse chestnut, maple, and other trees and shrubs that you like. Give away their seeds as gifts. It can become a regular project for your school or other organization and can supply your town with beautiful, free trees that are a delight to see and watch as they grow and grow over the years.

Another gardening project that would be of interest to some people in your town would be a garden show. The key to success in this kind of project is variety and the number of chances people have to win. It's not important that the prizes be large and expensive. It is important that there be enough categories and divisions so that a lot of people can win something.

Start out small. For example, make your first garden show for only one class in your school. Ask one or two of the science teachers to act as judges. Offer prizes for as many different kinds of plants as you can: best plants grown indoors, best plants grown outdoors, largest vegetable (that is, largest pumpkin, largest cabbage, largest squash, etc.), smallest dwarf tree, most colorful plant, most colorful flower, best bulb plants, and so on. Divide each category into people who have gardened before and people who are gardening for the first time. Give identical prizes to the winners in each group.

As we said before, prizes do not have to be expensive. Ribbons for first, second, and third place are available inexpensively in most towns or they can be ordered through the mail. Small plants, made from other plants and planted in pots that have been painted or wrapped in colorful aluminum foil, also make attractive, inexpensive prizes.

After you have one successful garden show to your credit you can enlarge it the following year to include some additional classes or even the whole school. As your reputation for wonderful garden shows grows year by year, you might even work out arrangements for competing with another school. The more people you can interest in gardening the better it will be.

In the preceding chapter we mentioned "forcing" bulbs into bloom. Most people immediately think of getting "ordinary" bulbs like tulips, daffodils, and hyacinths to bloom beautifully indoors. Few people think of forcing magnificent lilies into bloom and even fewer people realize they can get them to bloom exactly on the date they want. How about having some perfect lilies blooming beautifully indoors on Mother's Day or Easter Sunday? What could be nicer than presenting your mother, grandmother, or other relative or friend with a pot filled with such beauty? Here's how to go about it.

Decide in advance who the gift is for, when you want it to bloom, and what color or colors suit the occasion. Some of the colors you may choose include silver, gold, red, pink, white, crimson, yellow, and multicolored. Remember to keep it simple for the most attractive display.

To get the flowers to bloom right on time for that special occasion, simply find out how long it takes each variety to go from planting time to bloom and then figure backward. Hybrid lilies take about 70 days to bloom, oriental hybrids and speciosums take almost 120 days to bloom. Find the day you want your lilies to bloom and circle it on the calendar. Count back until you reach the total number of days your lily variety needs to go from planting to blooming. Circle this date on the calendar and remember to do your planting on that date. If, for example, you want to give the flowering gift on Valentine's Day (February 14), you would plant the hybrid variety of lily in early December.

Order your bulbs from a well-known mail-order house or pick them up at a local garden shop. If you order by mail, do it early enough to get the largest possible selection. Select the largest bulbs you can afford to buy. Though all but the smallest lily bulbs force well, the larger the bulb the more buds there will be to bloom. Store your bulbs in a paper bag in the refrigerator until you're ready to plant them. Don't put them in the coldest spot (near the coils) or in the freezer, but just in the refrigerator where they'll stay cool and dormant at about 34 to 40 degrees Fahrenheit.

When planting day arrives, take the bulbs out of cold storage and pot them in a mixture of potting soil and compost. Select a pretty pot that has a drain hole in the bottom. It can be made of anything that will hold soil and water—wood, plastic, ceramic, clay, or metal. Fill the pot about half full with the mixture and space the bulbs on top. Three or four bulbs fit nicely into a 6-inch pot. Cover the bulbs with between 2 and 3 inches of soil mixture and water thoroughly.

Put the pot in a sunny window that has a temperature of at least 65 degrees during the day and 55 degrees when the sun goes down. Water the plants often but, as we've said so many times before, don't drown them. When you are able to see growth, add some liquid organic fertilizer (fish emulsion is excellent) to the soil every two weeks according to the directions on the fertilizer container. Then there is nothing more to do but watch, wait, and look forward to the day that you'll present the gift.

CHAPTER 6

Outsmarting the Pests

They're all after the same thing you are. All the aphids, asparagus beetles, bagworms, borers, cabbage moths and worms, codling moths, cucumber beetles (you might have either striped or spotted), cutworms, Japanese beetles, leaf hoppers, miners or rollers, Mexican bean beetles, mites, nematodes, potato bugs, root maggots, scale crawlers, spider mites, thrips, tomato hornworms, wireworms, to name just a few, want just what you want—to enjoy the beautiful, lush produce you worked so hard to grow in your garden. They would like to eat the blooms and leaves of colorful flowers, would enjoy eating the tenderest, most delicious parts of your home-grown vegetables and fruits, and would love to wash it all down with the juices they suck from all kinds of plants. Allowed to run free, this assortment of insect pests would have a wonderful time, and after all your hard work, you'd have nothing.

Most people, faced with this situation, think "quick, kill all the insects before they kill all the plants." Then they run to get the spray gun, mix up a batch of awful smelling chemicals, and spray everything in sight—vegetables, fruits, trees, flowers, shrubs, and, of course, anything that flies or crawls. The result is more damage than anticipated: the insects, both the good and the bad, are dead, the balance of nature is upset, and everything, including those luscious fruits and vegetables, are covered with *poison*. Insecticides do not do the job the best way. Fortunately there is a better way— *nature's way*.

Nature has given us many ways to prevent disease and insects from ruining our gardens. Some of these ways are better than others. Some work almost all the time. Some work for some people on certain plants. Others work for other people on those same plants as well as on other plants. But they are all worth trying, until you find what is best for you.

The very first thing to learn and to practice is garden cleanliness. The cleaner you keep your garden the healthier your plants will be and, consequently, the opportunity for diseases to develop and insects to invade will be lessened. All the things you don't want in a garden—disease, bad insects, fungi—grow and multiply in filth and wetness. Sickly, diseased plants quickly become breeding grounds for unwanted guests.

Clean everything out of the garden that doesn't belong there. Pick up and get rid of all the leaves, vegetables, and fruits, as well as anything else lying around on the ground. If the things you pick up are clean and healthy, add them to your compost heap. If anything is slimy, buggy, or diseased, get rid of it, put it out with the garbage or have it burned. Keep an eye on your organic mulches. If left in place too long, they too can become breeding grounds for all sorts of insects and diseases. Start with fresh mulch each growing season. Pick up the mulch at the end of a single growing season and plow it under or add it to your compost heap.

One of the very easiest ways to prevent and avoid disease in a garden involves using your head long before you plant anything. Each year seedsmen and researchers develop plant varieties that are resistant to certain diseases and insects. The list gets longer and longer every year. The wise gardener takes advantage of this. By selecting only those special resistant varieties, gardeners are now able to grow plants that have a "built in" protection from many harmful diseases and insects. This is one time where man and nature have teamed up to produce something that's even better than nature could do alone.

When selecting your plants, there is something else to keep in mind. Certain plants will protect other plants from insects and even from chipmunks, moles, and mice. For example, a few cloves of garlic planted around the base of a peach tree will keep borers away. Planted in with raspberries, garlic will keep Japanese beetles from doing their usual damage. Planted with roses it helps keep both black spot and mildew from attacking. And, planted in other spots in the garden, garlic protects against aphids and several different kinds of beetles and also keeps mice, chipmunks, and other rodents away. Another "strong smeller," chives, does an excellent job of keeping aphids off roses, other flowers, lettuce, and peas. It's a matter of getting two for the price of one—insect repellent along with delicious, tangy vegetables, herbs, and spices.

Many other herbs and spices will also give you double service. Their strong smell will keep insects away from your plants and their wonderful taste and appeal will add much to your mom's cooking. Mints, almost any kind you can think of, but especially spearmint, will protect the cabbage family from harm. Place the mint plants in among the cauliflower, broccoli, Brussels sprouts, and, of course, cabbage, and the insects that would normally bother these plants will go somewhere else. Mint placed near and around the house will be a good protection against an ant invasion. The herb rosemary keeps cabbage moths and Mexican bean bettles from attacking in a vegetable garden. Rue will keep a great many insects off a great many flowers, vegetables, and even shrubs and trees. Tansy does a good job of protecting your plants from cabbage worms and cutworms. Thyme too helps to keep cabbage worms away. Basil, a special friend of tomatoes, not only keeps them free of both disease and insects but also tastes delicious when eaten with the fruit. Savory does a similar job when planted near most kinds of beans. Other herbs do similar jobs for other plants. Do some experimenting on your own—find out which ones work best for you.

Flowers also do more than just look pretty and many of them keep

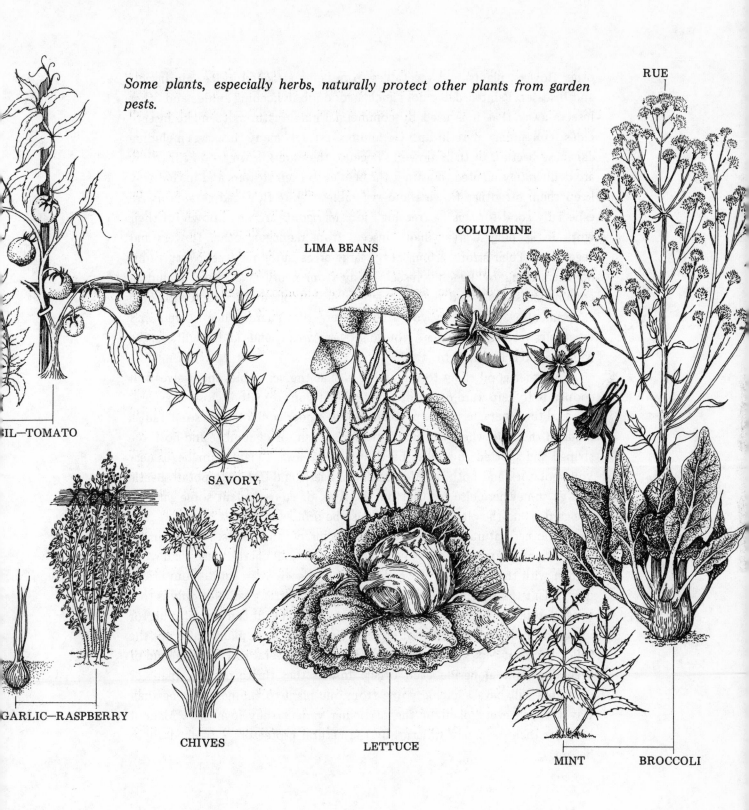

Some plants, especially herbs, naturally protect other plants from garden pests.

RUE

COLUMBINE

LIMA BEANS

SIL—TOMATO

SAVORY

GARLIC—RASPBERRY

CHIVES

LETTUCE

MINT

BROCCOLI

other flowers, plants, and vegetables from being attacked by certain insects and diseases. Painted daisy does such a good job in keeping aphids and other insects away that it is used by commercial manufacturers to make insecticides containing pyrethrum. Geraniums attract many insects, including Japanese beetles, to their flowers. Because they are known to do this, they are deliberately planted to attract the beetles to their flowers and in that way keep them off other flowers and vegetables. White flowered geraniums are especially good for this "attracting" job. Marigolds are well known for their work in keeping a great many insects from damaging other flowers and vegetables. Their strong aroma keeps large areas quite bug-free. Nasturtiums do their thing by keeping insects away from many vine crops, including cucumbers, squash, and melons. Here's another place for you to do some experimenting, and when you find flowers that guard other flowers and vegetables from insects, share your discovery with friends and neighbors. We will all appreciate the help.

Another good thing to remember is that the vegetables themselves will cooperate to help ward off garden pests. Plant your tomatoes close to asparagus and the asparagus beetle problem will be under control. Toss some radish seeds in the hole when you plant melon, squash, or cucumber and both the striped and spotted cucumber beetles will stay away. Plant your beans near your potatoes and both the Mexican bean beetle and Colorado potato beetle will go somewhere else for their meals. And, of course, plant some garlic in the garden and the plants nearby will also be protected against bugs.

Another natural way to prevent some insects and diseases from coming to visit and staying to ruin your garden is to outsmart them. Plan your garden with that in mind. Move things around each year; rotate your crops, don't plant the same thing in the same place year after year. Not only is that type of rotation better for the soil and the plants, but it is more difficult for insects as well. If you plant root crops in a spot one year, plant leaf crops the following year. Mix your crops too—don't plant several rows of one kind of vegetable right alongside each other. Insects that thrive on that plant or vegetable will have a picnic going from one plant to the next, eating their way through every plant of the particular variety they love best. Make it hard for them—separate varieties by the natural protectors we talked about before.

Keep the garden not only clean, but dry as well. Water belongs down with the roots, not in puddles on the surface. Plants left to sit in water attract diseases and insects. Plant your rows far apart so air can move around and between plants and dry the leaves and other plant parts. Be careful, fussy, and on the lookout. Make it as difficult for insects and diseases to get a start in your garden as you can. Plants grown indoors (or outdoors in containers) are also often attacked by pests. Cleanliness and frequent checking will usually keep them disease- and insect-free. If problems occur look into some of the suggestions made for outdoor gardens.

Speaking of checking, here is another excellent "control the problem measure," which could be called "watching not waiting." If you look often and know what you are looking for and are alert enough to spot trouble just as it starts, before it gets serious, you'll be way ahead of the game. Look at your plants, around your plants, and on your plants for any sign of trouble. Look every day. Check the tops and undersides of leaves, check buds and flowers, check all parts of vegetables and fruits as well as stalks and stems and the soil around the base of your plants.

Check for holes, curled leaves, spots, insect droppings, eggs, color changes, and anything else out of the ordinary. All of these things are sure signs of trouble. If you can find the trouble right at the beginning you've won about half the battle. The other half of the battle is to find out what is causing the trouble and get rid of it. Even though nature's balance will keep you trouble-free most of the time, there are those times when you must give nature a helping hand.

A clean, cold, strong water spray is one way to get insects off your plants. Don't waste water doing the job. Spot the enemy, squirt him, and move on to the next one. Once the harmful insects are on the ground you can either step on them or leave them, stunned, for their natural enemies. However, if you leave them, some will go right back to devouring your plants, while others, like aphids, will realize they are not welcome and go elsewhere for their next meal.

If the plain water is only partly successful and you feel you need something stronger, try adding a little soap or soap powder to the water spray. DO NOT USE DETERGENTS. A small amount of soap mixed with water will rid you of a variety of insect pests. If you've ever gotten a

Garden insects harmful to your plants.

A – STRIPED BLISTER BEETLE
B – ROSE LEAFHOPPER
C – JAPANESE BEETLE
D – ROSE APHID
E – MEXICAN BEAN BEETLE
F – HARLEQUIN CABBAGE BEETLE
G – SQUASH BUG
H – SPOTTED ASPARAGUS BEETLE
I – COLORADO POTATO BEETLE
J – STRIPED CUCUMBER BEETLE
K – CABBAGE MOTH
L – ASPARAGUS BEETLE
M – TWELVE SPOTTED CUCUMBER BEETLE
N – CUTWORM
O – SLUG
P – GRASSHOPPER

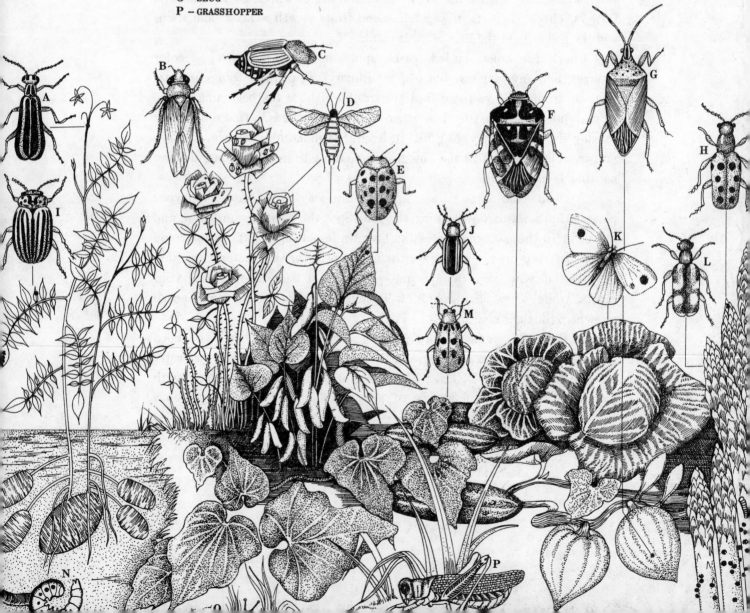

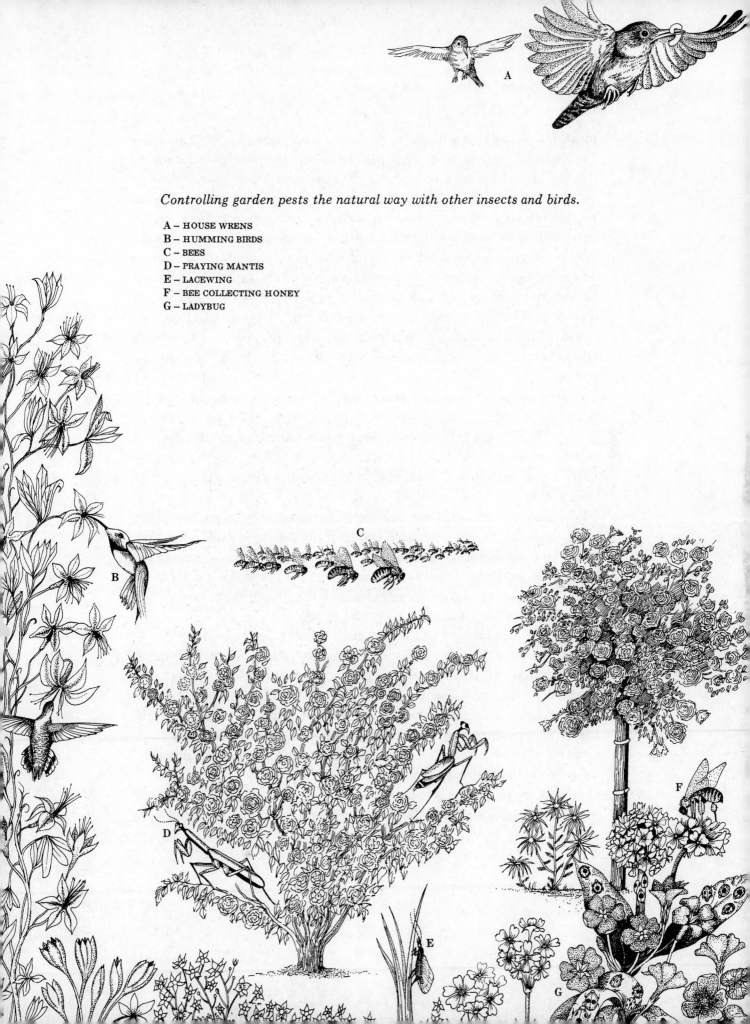

Controlling garden pests the natural way with other insects and birds.

A – HOUSE WRENS
B – HUMMING BIRDS
C – BEES
D – PRAYING MANTIS
E – LACEWING
F – BEE COLLECTING HONEY
G – LADYBUG

mouthful of soap, you'll know why the insects run. A couple of other "home-made" recipes work very well on insect pests and do no harm to flowers, vegetables, pets, or anything else. Ground tomato leaves soaked in water and made into a spray will eliminate aphids. Hot peppers do a good job against most insects that chew, including caterpillars, tomato worms, ants, spiders, and cabbage worms. Grind the pepper pods in a blender until they are liquid, add the same amount of water as you have pepper pod juice and a tablespoon or two of dishwasher soap liquid (to make it stick to the leaves). Mix it all together and spray it on your plants. An onion spray will do a similar job against spiders, aphids and others. Finely ground limestone mixed with water becomes whitewash, and when painted on a tree trunk (especially fruit trees) will protect the tree from insects that borrow into the tree.

Here are some more you might want or need to try: beer in a saucer, placed level with the soil, invites slugs to sip; they fall in get drunk and drown. Flour spread between rows stops cabbage worms and other harmful worms and slugs. The flour coats their skin and kills them. Molasses on a board turned sticky side down also invites insects to come and dine; they stick and die.

Corn is one crop that can be completely ruined by a single insect, the corn earworm, so be on the watch and be ready for them if and when they come. Once again there is a homemade, natural remedy ready to come to the rescue. Just as the silks start to turn brown, drip a few drops of mineral oil or castor oil on the part of the silk closest to the husk opening. Be sure you get it onto each ear's silk. This takes a lot of time, but see if it isn't worth it the first time you eat corn on the cob only minutes from the stalk.

There are still two more natural methods to use in controlling damage-causing insects and they're both probably the most fun to do and certainly the most fun to watch. Put friendly, helpful birds and insects to work, on a full-time basis, eating the "bad guys." What a great job those birds and insects have—eating all they want of the things they like best, all day long, seven days a week. How nice for the birds, ladybugs, praying mantises, lacewing flies, and trichogramma wasps.

Birds are probably the most cheerful, best looking, cheapest, and most successful insect gobblers to be found anywhere. And, not only will they work for peanuts or a handful of birdseed, they'll even whistle while they work. But they won't work on a regular, full-time basis for just anyone—only for their friends. To get to be their friend, you must take care of them all year long, not only when you need them. To get birds to come to your garden to work for you, you must give them food, places to nest, and safety from cats and other enemies. If there are trees with winter berries on your property, the birds will feel very welcome. In addition, put out food for them. Though they will probably not need the food to survive, it will come in handy when snow and ice covers the ground and trees and food is hard to find. More important, they become accustomed to coming to your property; they begin to know where they can get food when they need it. You can buy large bags of birdseed in supermarkets and in garden and nursery shops. If you want to give your future workers a special treat, put out some peanuts or peanut butter, suet, sunflower seeds, bits of fruit, bread, and an assortment of seeds and nuts. Start feeding in late fall and continue to feed regularly all through the winter and early spring. Stop feeding during the summer so that the birds, who are now used to coming to your property for food, will hunt for their own meals and consequently rid your garden of many pests.

To keep your bird workers happy, be sure an assortment of nesting materials is available. Sometimes nesting materials are a bit difficult to find and the birds have to travel some distance before they locate what they want. Make it a little easier for them by setting out some 6-inch pieces of string, thread, or cloth, some hay or straw, strands of wool, straw packing material, and even horse and human hair.

A few natural or specially built perches, a birdbath, and some dense brush to hide in also bring birds to your property. Is it worth all the trouble? Yes! Yes! Yes! For their songs. For their cheerfulness. For their color. And for their ability to eat *many pounds* of bugs every day. Some common birds eat at least 1,000 insects each day, while others eat as many as 5,000 daily. They're like living vacuum cleaners in the garden and are well worth your work in attracting them and tempting them to stay.

Other bug-gulping vacuum cleaners, but on a smaller scale, are the predator insects, the ones that eat other insects. You've probably heard that you are not supposed to harm ladybugs or praying mantises and now you know why. They are insects that do a lot of good and no harm. Along with a few other insects, they eat no vegetables or flowers but, instead, eat the insects that do.

Ladybugs do a fantastic job on such pests as aphids, whiteflies, spider mites, and mealybugs, and when these insects are scarce, they will go after other harmful bugs in the garden. Each fully grown ladybug eats about fifty aphids a day. Can you imagine what a job several dozen would do for your garden and you? To help you get enough of them to really clean out your garden, several companies raise them and sell them through the mail. Buy them for your garden, follow the directions on the package, release them in the spring in the early evening, and they'll go right to work for you. All they ask are plenty of bugs to eat. For your kindness they and their children will come back each year for many, many years.

Another larger, fiercer looking predator, the praying mantis, will also work for you. While they are young, mantises go after soft insects like aphids, but once they grow up they eat caterpillars, crickets, chinch bugs, beetles, flies, and many other pests. Mantises too can bought from companies that raise them. They come in egg cases, which must be tied securely to a tree limb or shrub branch. Each egg mass contains about one hundred mantises, which hatch in late spring. Not all the insects survive, of course, but those that do eat and eat and eat. The female lays eggs, and your own supply will hatch the following year.

Another group of helpful insects, the parasites, are also very useful, eating the eggs and larvae before they even have a chance to hatch. The best known and easiest to buy are the lacewing flies and the trichogramma wasps, both of which can become very valuable workers (even though unseen) in your garden.

With all these different and excellent ways of controlling insect pests and diseases, your garden should be both fun and productive. You should be able to grow many beautiful plants and flowers and delicious vegetables without ever having to use any chemical poisons or killers. The natural way is a much better way.

CHAPTER 7

Timing Makes the Difference

By now you can see that organic gardening is for everyone—young or old, rich or poor, girl or boy. It is also for every time—spring, summer, fall, and winter. The more you do, the more and better your results will be. The earlier you plan and then prepare, the more successful you'll be with everything you try. Here are some suggestions for every month of the year. You can do as much or as little as you want. It's all up to you. Just remember, you get out only what you put in and that goes for all things and all months.

JANUARY

You can tell it's January without even looking at the calendar. Look, instead, in the mailbox. January is the month the seed catalogs arrive. Now's the time to start looking and planning, while outdoor gardening seems far away. Carefully go through the catalogs and list the flowers, fruits, and vegetables you want to grow in the coming season. Don't trust your memory, put everything down on paper.

Check the descriptions in the seed catalogs to be certain you know exactly what you are getting, how they will grow, the colors, sizes, and shapes. Check also to be sure your climate is good for the plants you want to grow. Areas that are too hot, too cold, or get too much or too little rain are good for some plants and not good for others. Try to select those plants that have the best chance of "making it" in your area. Also plan to order one plant or variety you've never grown just so you can try it.

Once you've done all your planning, figuring, and charting, take the next step—order. Don't wait, it doesn't pay. All the advantages of early ordering far outweigh any real or imagined disadvantages. Make up your mind, write up the order, and get ready for another year full of gardening adventures.

FEBRUARY

If you've done your job in January, you'll have plenty to do in February. The seeds you ordered should arrive some time during the month so you can get started with your seedlings. And, if you take a look at the calendar, you'll notice that some bulbs forced into action late this month will come into their full blooming glory just in time for Mother's Day.

When your seeds arrive from the mail order company or you pick them up at your favorite garden store, check each package to make sure you've received exactly what you wanted. Check too to see that the seeds are fresh, packed for the year in which they are to be planted. Read and pay attention to all the information and suggestions on the packages. If you've received live planting materials, such as bulbs, roots, plants, or others, open their packages, make sure they've arrived in good condition and haven't dried out. Do whatever the planting instructions (packed with the material) say should be done with these materials if they must wait a while before being planted.

Start seedlings for all those flowers and vegetables that need eight to ten weeks in the house before they can be transplanted outside to your cold frame for hardening off. Don't rush. The last week of the month is usually the best time for such vegetables as tomatoes, melons, cucumbers, cabbage, and peppers.

MARCH

Your sitting days are over. By the time the winds of March have started to wane you should have started all the seedlings you intend to start, read all the garden books you intend to read, forced all the bulbs you intended to force, and planned all the plans you intended to plan. Once all these are done the real action part of gardening begins.

Not many sprays are recommended for use by organic gardeners. The one commercially prepared exception is a dormant oil spray and March is the month to do the job. Dormant oil spray is a spray made of oil (3 percent, a very small amount of oil) that is sprayed on trees and shrubs while they are dormant—before the buds open and the leaves start to grow. A whole list of chewing and sucking insects can be controlled by this spray, including aphids, red spiders, thrips, mealybugs, scale insects, and mites. The spray is harmless to the trees (if you put on too much it just runs off) and to just about everything else as well. It controls the insects by coating them with oil before they can hatch. Buy commercially prepared pure dormant oil spray (not lime-sulphur or other sprays that include poisonous mixtures with it) and on the first day the temperature goes over 40 degrees, get out there with your fellow organic gardeners and do some preventive spraying.

Watch for some early hardy bulbs to bloom with the welcome message that spring can't be too far away.

APRIL

Here we go. Get the shovel. As soon as the soil has dried enough so that you aren't turning over mud, start turning over the area for your garden. If you started a compost heap last year, take the completed compost and start working it into the soil as you dig.

You can even do some planting this month. Onions, cabbage, lettuce, and some very early flowers like the cool weather, so get them into the ground this month for best growth.

You'll be able to tell it's time for the earliest spring planting when your favorite spring flowering bulbs make their appearance. While they bloom they are beautiful, but when only the leaves are left, the area is a mess. True organic gardeners shrug their shoulders and say "that's nature." If you're a neatness nut, tie each bulb's leaves with a piece of string or a rubber band to tidy things up. Don't cut or tear off the leaves; they are working with the bulbs to produce and store food for next year's blooms.

Watch the buds start to open and the flowers form—all of nature is coming back to life. Notice how each tree does its own thing. When the pin oaks finally shed last year's brown leaves and replace them with new, young, green leaves, spring is definitely here to stay.

MAY

If you haven't done so already, remove all protective coverings from plants, trees, and shrubs. Don't actually put them away yet; there might very well be a few freezing nights left and you'll need them again.

Get the seedlings that are scheduled to go into the garden into the cold frame for hardening off. Don't put them in there and forget about them. Watch them carefully. As the temperature rises during the day remove the cover. Just before the sun goes down in the evening (when it can get quite cold) replace the cover and leave it there overnight. Also watch the seedlings to make sure the plants don't dry out. Water when necessary.

As you get closer and closer to Memorial Day you also get closer and closer to the time when almost all but the tenderest of plants can go into the garden. Check to see that all planting areas have been prepared and are ready to receive seedlings. Also, as the last week of the month approaches, start sowing all the seed that goes directly into the ground.

The flowering trees will tell you when it's time to get your vegetables and flowers into the garden. Watch for their beautiful signal and you can't miss on your timing.

JUNE

This is the start of giving and taking time. If you planted strawberries last year you can start picking some of the biggest, juiciest strawberries you ever saw. Eat 'em raw, eat 'em cooked, eat 'em alone, and eat 'em with something. No matter how you eat them, you're in for a real treat. (That's an extra bonus of organic gardening. When you garden without poisons you don't have to resist the temptation to pick one—eat one, pick one—eat one.)

Keep the plants weeded and mulched well and add some compost along the rows. This is a good time to start a fresh compost heap so you'll have a good supply when it's time to turn the garden over at the end of the growing season. Ideally, that is if you have the space, you should have three separate compost heaps. One should be the new one you're making now, the second should be a "working" pile (actively turning all the organic matter you can give it into compost), and the third should be beautiful, crumbly, rich compost, ready to be spread where it will do the most good as you need it.

Keep a close eye on your early planted vegetables. Some should be ready for picking. Never allow produce to stay in the garden "an extra day or two so it gets real big." Garden fresh produce is at its best and tastes best when it is very young and very, very tender. That's one of the main advantages of having your own garden—all the produce can be picked at the peak of its perfect best.

Thin out all the vegetables you started from seed directly in the garden. But don't throw away the ones you pull out; use them in salads and as interesting fresh vegetables—you may be surprised and pleased at the taste.

Move as many houseplants outside as you can. Keep them well watered—every day, two or three times a day if necessary.

JULY

Some harvesting, some watering, some weeding, and a lot of watching. That's the plan for this usually hot month.

You'll be able to pick lettuce, cabbage, carrots, onions, cucumbers, a few tomatoes (toward the end of the month), loads of green beans, radishes, green peas, broccoli, Brussels sprouts, and more (if you planted them). Don't be left out of the fun next year—plant your favorites from among these, on time, and join us next year. Make a note for next year's planting of those you might have forgotten and those that were especially successful.

This month is a very important maintenance month. There's no more

April is the time to prepare the garden for new seedlings by digging up the soil and working in compost.

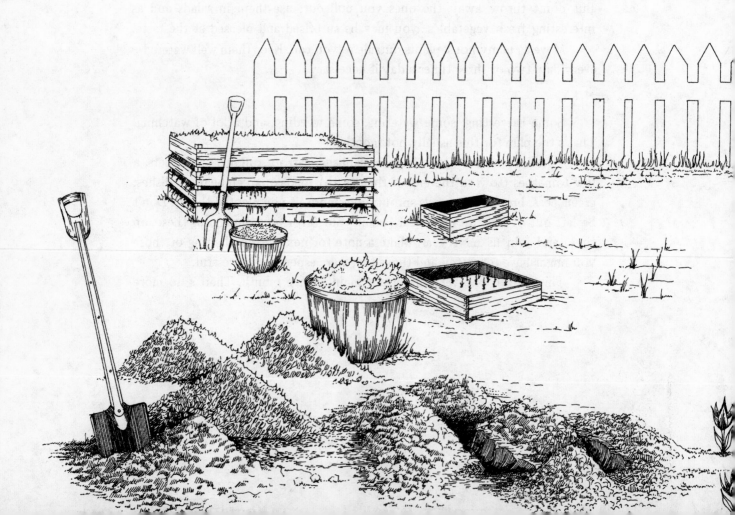

Spring is also the time when the bulbs you planted last fall burst into bloom.

A – "ATHLEET" (MENDEL TULIP)
B – "GOLDEN AGE" (DARWIN TULIP)
C – "FANTASY" (PARROT TULIP)
D – "PINK GEM" (MENDEL TULIP)
E – "BRILLIANT STAR" (SINGLE EARLY TULIP)
F – "CROMARTY" (TRUMPET NARCISSUS)
G – WATERLILY TULIP (*kaufmanniana*)
H – HYACINTHS (*hyacinthus*)
I – "MARCELLINA" (COTTAGE TULIP)
J – GREIG TULIP (*greigii*)
K – FOSTER TULIP (*fosteriana*)
L – WATIER JONQUIL (*watieri*)
M – GLORY-OF-THE SNOW (*chionodoxa*)
N – CLOTH-OF-GOLD CROCUS (*susianus*)
O – COMMON CROCUS (*vernus*)
P – GRAPE HYACINTH (*muscari*)

planting or transplanting and little else besides making certain that all your plants have what they need to live and thrive. The hot weather dries everything out very quickly, so watch your watering. Always water well, never sprinkle. Though everyone has his own idea about the best time to water, some things just make good sense. If you water at night some plants will go to sleep with wet feet because the soil won't dry quickly without the warm sun. If you water during the hottest part of the day the soil dries too quickly under the hot sun. That leaves early morning as probably the best time to water. Do as we did, try them all and see for yourself.

Watch the weeds this month too. Add mulch wherever needed to keep the weeds down and pull any weeds that sneak through the mulch. Weeds are plants that fight your plants for the food in the soil. Pulling them out means your plants will have more room to grow and more opportunity to get a proper diet from the soil.

Remember to keep an eye on all the houseplants that have been moved outside and water them several times a day if necessary.

AUGUST

This is a "more of the same" kind of month. You must keep watching, watering, and weeding all through the month. This is made a lot easier by the amount of harvesting you'll be doing. It reaches a peak at this time. To everything else you have been harvesting, you can now add lots and lots of flowers, tomatoes, peppers, eggplant, melons, and just about everything else you have growing in your garden. Check the garden at least once a day or some vegetables will grow too big or may even spoil. Do your picking when it's cool outside and when there is no moisture on the leaves (from watering, rain, or dew). In most cases this "best time" is in early evening.

Do a little thinking about the time vacation will be over and you will be going back to school. Plan to take some green, growing things with you. Select a few special plants that can be transplanted and take them to school with you. Do the same for your house, of course, so you can have some beautiful houseplants for the winter.

Don't watch the clock, watch the sun. Early morning and late evening are the best time to do your gardening work. Best for you and best for the

The end of the summer is time to harvest. Melons, carrots, onions, peppers, beets, egg plant, squashes, cabbage, celery, beans, lettuce, and tomatoes are the rewards of your gardening.

plants. Use the hottest parts of the day for cool activities and the coolest part of the day for gardening.

SEPTEMBER

Harvesting continues, and thoughts of approaching cool weather now begin to affect your working and planning. Keep picking daily for as long as you can. When you get more than you can eat of one fruit or vegetable, freeze or preserve them. Work with your parents (both mom and dad will enjoy this activity) to "put up" some of your home-grown produce. Follow the directions exactly as given in the freezing and preserving books and you'll be able to taste and enjoy the produce of summer all year long.

Start moving plants that will be damaged by cold weather back indoors. Don't put off for tomorrow what you had better do today. There is usually little or no warning of a cold snap and once it comes it's too late. A few minutes taken right now, before the first nighttime frost, and you will be sure to have all your plants thriving in good health throughout the long winter.

Play a game of bulb switching. Take all the summer flowering bulbs out of the ground and store them. Put all your spring flowering bulbs into the ground exactly where you want them to grow next year.

Watch for the start of the chrysanthemum display and you'll know for sure that fall is here.

OCTOBER

Most of the gardening is done for the year. Now it's time to start preparing for next year. Turn your compost pile after adding all the manure and organic matter that you can find. Turn over the garden soil and leave it in large lumps or clods just as it comes off the spade. The sun, wind, rain, ice, and freezing and thawing works on the soil, gets rid of some insects, and gives you better soil for the next garden season.

Clean up all around your garden. Anything that can be turned into compost should be added to the pile. Anything that is diseased or insect-ridden should be put out with the trash. Start looking for loads of leaves from neighbors and friends to add to your compost heap. Do yourself and them a favor by taking the leaves off their hands.

Make sure everything is ready for winter. Add extra mulch to places where extra protection is needed. A few sticks or stones will keep it in place in windy locations.

Turn your attention indoors and get back to working in earnest with your indoor plants.

NOVEMBER

Think about the people you know and love who deserve very special plant gifts. Try to match the plant to the person—colorful plants to colorful people, greenery for more quiet and formal people. Repot houseplants in larger pots, using your favorite potting soil mixture (potting soil and compost). Remember to drop a piece of broken clay pot in the bottom first, to cover the drain hole, then a piece of charcoal, then the potting mixture, the plant, and more potting soil mix. Decorate the pot with natural materials—pine cones, grasses, dried flowers, pretty weeds—and set it aside until gift-giving time. Make sure you have enough gifts to go around—everyone loves a live gift that shows thought and imagination.

DECEMBER

Look back on the year that has just passed and begin to look forward to the one that's coming up. Think about all the things that went right and all the things that went wrong. Make notes on what to do and what not to do next year. Send for seed and nursery catalogs, price lists, and brochures. Go to your local library and browse through the many garden books on the shelves. Try some of the general ones and some that cover only a single topic. Read and learn as much as you can so that the next time you garden naturally you will have the best time you ever had, naturally.

Glossary of Gardening Terms

annual — a plant, grown from seed, that completes a full life cycle—seed to flower to seed—in a single year and then dies

biennial — a plant that completes a full life cycle in more than one year but less than two years and then dies

blocking — cutting a seedling flat apart so that it is divided into cubes of seedlings, roots, and soil ready for transplanting

bulb — an underground stem made up of layers of scales attached to a disk from which shoots grow up and roots grow down

cold frame — a boxlike unit sunk partially in the ground and covered with a slanting top of glass or heavy sheet of plastic, used to start, harden off, protect, and grow some plants especially during early spring and late fall

compost — *see* humus

dibble — a pointy stick or tool used by gardeners to make small holes and for other transplanting purposes

dormant — being inactive for a period of time, such as plants and trees, after which growth begins again

dwarf — special trees or plants developed to grow smaller-than-normal varieties of the same plant

fertilizer — material, either chemical or organic, that is added to the soil to provide food for all kinds of trees, plants, and shrubs

forcing — inducing plants to grow or bloom when they normally wouldn't by using artificial means such as light or heat

fungi — members of a group of living things, including mushrooms, mildew, and mold, that live on living or dead organic matter and do not have the chlorophyll that gives green color to plants

fungicide — any of the many different chemical mixtures that either kill or stop the growth of fungi and spores

germinate — starting to grow and develop; in the case of plants, germination is indicated by the start of shoots or roots

growing cubes — *see* peat pots.

harden off	the process used by a gardener to get plants used to life outdoors, usually after they have been indoors for a while
hardy	plants and bulbs that can grow outdoors or remain outdoors all year long without any special protection
humus	decayed or almost decayed organic materials that become rich, black soil
life cycle	a complete life-death circle; in plants, from seed to plant to flower and back to seed
miticide	any of the different chemical mixtures that destroys mites
mulching	a protective cover placed over the soil and used to keep out weeds, catch rainwater, and for other purposes; can be organic hay, straw, grass clippings, pine bark, peat moss, or inorganic plastic, stones, aluminum, and others
parasite	a living thing that gets everything it needs by living off another living thing
peat pots	pots made of peat moss which are planted as a unit, plant, soil, and pot at one time (growing cubes are much the same); seeds can be started in them or seedlings transplanted to them, later to be planted in the garden when the young plant is big enough
perennial	plants that have life cycles that continue for at least two years
pollination	the act of getting pollen from parts of one plant to similar parts of another; usually needed to produce fruit but not needed to produce flowers
predator	an animal or insect that preys on other animals or insects on a regular basis for food
tender	plants and bulbs that will be damaged by the normal cold weather or frost found in certain parts of the country; usually best to either protect or move these plants indoors for the winter
thinning	pulling up and discarding all but the strongest seedlings
transplanting	to take a plant, tree, or shrub from one place and plant it in another place

Other Books to Read

Fenten, Barbara and D.X. *The Organic Grow it, Cook it, Preserve it Guidebook.* Grosset and Dunlap, New York, 1972.

Hunter, Beatrice Trum. *Gardening Without Poisons*, 2nd Edition. Houghton Mifflin Company, Boston, 1971.

Organic Gardening and Farming Magazine. *The Complete Book of Composting.* Rodale Press Inc., Emmaus, Pa. 1971.

Rodale, Robert, editor. *The Basic Book of Organic Gardening.* Ballentine Books, New York, 1971.

Stout, Ruth. *The Ruth Stout No Work Garden Book.* Rodale Press, Emmaus, Pa., 1971.

Sunset Books. *Sunset Guide to Organic Gardening.* Lane Books, Menlo Park, Calif., 1971.

Tyler, Hamilton. *Organic Gardening Without Poisons.* Van Nostrand Reinhold Company, New York, 1970.

List of Organic Gardening Suppliers

Armstrong Nurseries, Incorporated
Box 473
Ontario, California 91764

Asgrow-Mandeville Seed Company
15 W. Main Street
Cambridge, New York 12816

Ball, Incorporated, George I.
Post Office Box 335
West Chicago, Illinois 60185

Buntings' Nurseries, Incorporated
Box 3
Selbyville, Delaware 19975

Burpee, W. Atlee Company
Ford Hook Farms
Doylestown, Pennsylvania 19132

Crosman Seed Corporation
Crosman Terrace & West Commercial
East Rochester, New York 14445

Conard-Pyle Co. The
West Grove, PA 19390

Drybread Podocarpus
   Nursery
350 N.W. 161 St.
Miami, FLA 33169

Emlong Nurseries, Inc.
Stevensville, MI 49127

Ferry-Morse Seed Co.
P.O. Box 100
Mountain View,
CA 94042

Field, Henry, Seed
   & Nursery Co.
407 Sycamore
Shenandoah, IA 51601

Germain's, Inc.
4820 E. 50th St.
Los Angeles, CA 90058

Grootendorst, A.M. Inc.
P.O. Box 123
Benton Harbor,
MI 49022

Holland Bulb Co.
10420 S.E. 82nd
   Avenue
Portland, OR 97266

Howard's of Hemet
Hemet, CA 92343

Ilgenfritz Nurseries, Inc.
P.O. Box 665
Monroe, MI 48161

Jackson & Perkins Co.
P.O. Box 1028
Medford, OR 97501

Kelly Bros.
   Nurseries, Inc.
Box 430,
23 Maple Street
Dansville, NY 14437

Lake Womack Nursery
200 Oakdale
Manchester, TN 37355

Mandeville & King
P.O. Box 134
Rochester, NY 14601

Monrovia Nursery Co.
18331 E. Foothill Blvd.
P.O. Box Q
Azusa, CA 91702

Norganic Foods Co.
545 S. Clarence
Los Angeles, CA 90033

Northrup King & Co.
1500 Jackson St., N.E.
Minneapolis, MN 55413

Oak Grove Nurseries
Thomasville, GA 31792

Oregon Bulb Farms, Inc.
P.O. Box 529
Gresham, OR 97030

Pan-American Seed Co.
Box 438
West Chicago, IL 60185

Park, George W., Seed Co.
Greenwood, SC 29646

Rosedale Nurseries, Inc.
Hawthorne, NY 10532

Shenandoah Nurseries
Shenandoah, IA 51601

Spring Hill Nurseries Co.
Tipp City, OH 44077

Star Nurseries, Inc.
P.O. 372
Johnson Creek, WI 53038

Stark Bros. Nursery
Louisiana, MO 63353

Stern's Nurseries, Inc.
404 Williams St.
Geneva, NY 14456

Tennessee Valley Nursery, Inc.
Winchester, TN 37398

Union Nursery, Inc.
16420 S. Avalon Blvd.
Gardena, CA 90247

Van Bourgondien, K. & Sons
Farmingdale Road
P.O. Box A
Babylon, NY 11702

Vaughan's Seed Co.
5300 Katrine Ave.
Downers Grove, IL 60515

Wayside Gardens Co., The
9470 Mentor Avenue
Mentor, OH 44060

Index

Jonquill, 45, 47, 77

Lantana, 19
Larkspur, 37, 38, 40
Lettuce, 26, 28, 33, 62
Lily, 58-59
Limestone, 8-9, 30; whitewash, 68
Lupine, annual, 37, 39, 40; perennial, 43

Manure, 8, 25, 37
Marigolds, 14, 15, 37, 38, 40, 64
Meadowrue, 42, 43
Melon, 14, 15, 26, 27, 33, 64; watermelon, 34
Monkshood, 42, 43
Morning glory, 38, 40
Mulch, 37, 50-53, 61; nonorganic, 50, 53; organic, 50, 52, 61

Oak tree, 55-56
Onion, 26, 29, 31, 34; onion sets, 31
Orange, dwarf, 14
Organic gardening, 1-2, 50-51, 61, 75

Peas, 14, 15, 16, 26, 28, 31, 34, 62
Peat moss, 16, 46
Pepper, 15, 26, 33; hot, 68
Perennials, 36, 41-44, *see* name varieties
Petunia, 37, 38, 40
Phlox, annual, 39, 40; perennial, 42, 43
Plantain lily, 42, 44
Poppy, 37, 39, 40
Portulaca, 37, 39, 40
Potassium, 6, 7
Potato, 26, 29, 31-32, 34, 64
Primrose, 42, 43
Pumpkin, 14, 15, 26, 27, 33

Radish, 26, 30-31, 34, 64
Rhizome, 36, 45
Rhubarb, 29, 32, 34

Rose, 14, 15
Rudbeckia, 39, 40

Seed flats, 16
Seedling, 15-18, 23-25, 26, 27, 42, 51, 57, 72-73, 74
Seeds, 15, 26, 27, 37, 42, 56, 72, 74; "resistant," 61-62
Snapdragon, 37, 38, 41
Soil, 8; preparation, 8; seeding starting soil, 16
Soil structure, 3; adobe soil, 5; clay soil, 5; loamy soil, 3-5; sandy soil, 5
Speedwell, 42, 44
Spider plant, 19
Spinach, 26, 31, 34
Sprays, organic, 65, 68, 73
Squash, 26, 27, 33, 34, 64
Staking, 53, 57
Stock, 39, 40
Strawflower, 37, 38, 41
Sunflower, 38, 40
Sweet Alyssum, annual, 37, 38, 40; perennial, 43

Tomato, 17, 26, 28, 33, 34, 64; herb protectors for, 62; staking, 53
Training, 27, 53
Transplanting, 18, 23-26, 42-43, 51, 57
Trenching, 32
Trowel, 25
Tubers, 36, 45

Vegetables, 15, 26-34, 75, 76, 79; *see* name varieties
Virginia bluebell, 42, 43

Watering, 12, 42, 78
Weeding, 51, 78
Window box, 18, 19

Zinnia, 37, 38, 40

About the Author

D. X. Fenten began gardening as a weekend project in his backyard. His hobby has led to a yard filled with organically grown fruits, vegetables, and flowers, and to writing a number of books on gardening, garden photography, organic foods and how to grow them. He is the author of the children's book, *Plants for Pots: Projects for Indoor Gardeners*, and with his wife Barbara, is now writing a guide to natural foods for young readers.

Mr. Fenten was born and grew up in New York City and lives on Long Island with his wife and two children. He has B.A. and M.A. degrees from New York University and teaches writing, communications, and cinematography to high school students.

About the Artist

Howard Berelson was born in Brooklyn, New York, attended Pratt Institute there, and now makes his home in Brooklyn. He has illustrated several children's books and has had a show of his sculpture.